waters of BAPTISM

A BIBLE STUDY MEDIA SMALL GROUP STUDY

REV. WESLEY ARNING

© 2023 Wesley Arning

All rights reserved.

Published in Jacksonville, Florida by Bible Study Media, Inc.
Cover and Interior design by Shelby Dinkel of Dinkel Digital, LLC.

ISBN # 978-1-942243-66-3
Library of Congress Control Number: 2023900309

No part of this publication may be reproduced, stored in a retrieval system, or transmitted in any form or by any means electronic, mechanical, photocopy, recording, or otherwise except for brief quotations in printed reviews, without the prior written permission of the publisher.
www.biblestudymedia.com.

All Scripture quotations are from the ESV® Bible (The Holy Bible, English Standard Version®), copyright © 2001 by Crossway, a publishing ministry of Good News Publishers. Used by permission.
All rights reserved.

Printed in the United States of America.

To Megan who had to hear over the past year too many times, "I need to go work on my book."
Thank you for your constant love and support.

table of CONTENTS

6	**INTRODUCTION**
8	*week 1* **PRACTICING RIGHTEOUSNESS**
24	*week 2* **TEMPTATION AND REPENTANCE**
40	*week 3* **BE BORN AGAIN**
56	*week 4* **LIVING WATER**
72	*week 5* **NEW EYES**
88	*week 6* **DEATH TO LIFE**
104	**STUDY GUIDE**

introduction

Millions of art lovers, history buffs, and religious pilgrims pour into Florence yearly to experience all this Italian city offers. They come from around the globe to see Michelangelo's famous statue of David or shop in some of Europe's most glamorous stores. Its treasure-trove of food, art, and culture is unequaled. There is no other city like it.

Each morning, locals and tourists pour into the streets like ants, with the smell of espresso in the air. Some are off to work while others get in line at the Uffizi Art Gallery before it opens. No matter where they head, it seems all the streets lead to the Piazza del Duomo—the city's magnetic center, which is how the original designers wanted it. Unknown to many visitors, they turn a corner, and there at the center of the piazza is the massive Cathedral of Santa Maria, known for being one of the Renaissance's prized jewels. It is a sight to behold in beauty and sheer size.

Like bees around a hive, people buzz around the Cathedral as if it has its own gravitational force. With this flurry of activity, many may not notice the smaller, octagonal building across the way known as the Baptistery. Some say that on that site, a temple was once dedicated to Mars, the Roman god of war. It seems fitting that on that same site, people for over a millennium have been baptized into the Prince of Peace's sacrificial death and glorious resurrection.

From the earliest days of the Christian movement, baptism had a central function. Typically, men and women spent two or three years preparing for their baptism in the catechumenate process. During that time, they were instructed in the faith and dedicated themselves to fasting and prayer. This long journey culminated in the Easter Vigil, where they were led to a private room to remove their clothes (to signify the new birth they were about to receive) and a deacon baptized them. They were then led into the main church where the whole Christian community greeted them, and a bishop anointed them with oil. Then they were invited into the Easter celebration, each as a full church member, to receive communion for the first time.

When my wife and I visited Florence a few years ago, I imagined all the newly baptized who had processed by candlelight from the Baptistery to the Cathedral over the centuries. Young and old, rich and poor, male and female walking the well-worn path from the font to the Lord's Table. When those massive doors opened during the Easter Vigil service, and the newly baptized saw the great crowd anxiously awaiting their arrival, they must have realized they were no longer students of the faith; they were now family.

Jesus' great commission to his apostles after his resurrection was to go into all the world to preach, teach, and baptize in the name of Father, Son, and Holy Spirit. From the beginning, baptism has been understood as the doorway into this new family.

The assigned Gospel lessons in this book will help us sort out what Jesus expects of this new family with its origin and purpose in him. The baptized are called into a new life of faith requiring a certain lifestyle. We will begin on a practical level with passages from Matthew and move on to the Gospel of John where we will see shining examples of faith.

I pray this book will be a helpful resource to those seeking the sacrament of baptism, or those who want to explore its meaning further. Though we will look at each passage in-depth, baptismal living is a core theme that undergirds the whole work. I pray this adventure into **the great themes of baptism might** be as fruitful for you as it has been for me.

Wesley Laming

week 1
PRACTICING RIGHTEOUSNESS

Day 1 • MATTHEW 6:1-4

"What about the works?" This was the consistent reply from a member of a Bible study I attended years ago. "Faith is good and all, but what about the works?" I guess he had seen too many Christians who said one thing and did another. In those Bible study sessions, he never wanted our discussions to be spiritualized to where they had no implication for our daily life. There was work to be done!

Those discussions were quite helpful, and yet I'm dumbfounded that we're struggling with the idea of faith and works as if the Reformation happened only yesterday. The church has rich answers to these tough questions, but the pervasive anxiety, even in the pews today, only proves how hard it is to live out our faith. We desperately want to know what God requires of us. We see the fruit of God's kingdom throughout the Gospels, and Jesus expects his followers to bear fruit.

But what does that really mean?

"What about the works?"

Thankfully, Jesus hints at what kind of works are expected in our Gospel lesson and the pitfalls we will encounter. Like a choreographer, he shows us there is a dance between ourselves and the Gospel actions we are to live out. In our passage from Matthew 6, he doesn't warn us how we should embody our faith or live out our convictions, but how to "practice our righteousness." The dance of faith and works is all about embodying righteousness.

When the dance is going well, we notice the needy in our midst and help them secure their basic needs. Jesus doesn't say *if* you give to the needy but *when*. This dance includes others. It requires we have our eyes open to those around us and respond to their needs.

But Jesus takes it one step further: practicing our righteousness requires great secrecy. This will be a theme throughout this chapter, and I will consistently repeat it because Jesus knows we can't help but talk about the good work we do. There is a great line in J. D. Salinger's *The Catcher in the Rye* in which Holden Caulfield says, "If you do something good, then after a while, if you don't watch it, you start showing off. And then you're not good anymore."[1]

---

[1] J. D. Salinger, *The Catcher in the Rye* (Boston: Little Brown and Company, 1951), 164.

Even for a Christian, there is a danger to doing good—a fine line between a genuine act of charity and an opportunity for self-glorification. This is where the dance gets tricky. We stumble over our pride as we practice righteousness. There is just something so wonderful about doing good that it can become addictive. Like any addiction, something that may be harmless, even good for us, is consumed by our appetite for it. It becomes solely about us and our desires. Learning this intricate dance of righteousness—or right-living—takes discipline.

Jesus' call for covertness goes against everything our social media driven culture encourages. Self-promotion is the name of the game. We love posting about every aspect of our life. Our sense of self-worth increases with every new follower or like we receive. Social media has a whole category for "humble brags" where people will say something that appears self-deprecating while bringing attention to themselves. We are simply a product of the culture we have created.

Regarding this passage, we no longer must go to the synagogue or in the streets for others to praise us. We can now receive praise while sitting on our couch. The opportunity for self-glorification has become easier and more insidious since Jesus' time. The answer is not to stop doing good, but to be attentive to our underlying intentions and desires.

Like learning a new dance routine, one must take steps and keep disciplines to master this Gospel art form. In doing so, Jesus also challenges us to unlearn those things that make us stumble over ourselves. This Jesus dance is one of humility and care we must weave into our daily lives.
And so, shall we dance?

Reflection: What does practicing righteousness mean to you? How have you navigated the tough balance of faith and works?

Day 2 • MATTHEW 6:5-6

The first time I visited Jerusalem, the various forms of prayer I encountered struck me. As you walk from one religious quarter to the next, you may hear monks chanting in a church, young yeshiva boys rocking their bodies as they softly pray in front of the Western Wall, or shopkeepers kneeling on their mats as you walk through their stores during the call to prayer. The city is steeped in prayerful devotion.

Prayer is inherently good, just like giving to the poor in yesterday's reading. But Jesus, yet again, is concerned with *how* believers pray. Revealing how a person prays, Jesus believes, is a good indicator of the spirit behind their prayers.

In Jesus' time, the rabbis had passed down an old rule that forbade a person to pray loudly in public.[2] Ironically, some looked at the rule and said, "I guess that means we're allowed to pray *quietly* in public." Either way, it was a public endeavor. It may have been a genuine opportunity to talk to the Lord, but there was always the opportunity to be seen by others. And one thing Jesus is adamant about in this chapter is the only one who should see our religious devotion is the One we cannot see.

Fast forward to the present day. The first prayer a priest says in an Episcopal Sunday service is, "Almighty God, to you all hearts are open, all desires known, and from you no secrets are hid."[3] This prayer reminds us everything is laid before God. There are no surprises and no need to cover up our brokenness by attempting to impress our peers with flashy actions or loud prayers. God already knows. As scary as that may seem, it is meant to be comforting. We can stop pretending and come before God with an honest and sincere heart.

As a child, I took this passage literally. I would close my bedroom door, lock it, and quietly sit in the corner of my room. I didn't really know what to pray, so I'd sit there hoping God would notice I had followed the command for secrecy. After all, Jesus said God sees in secret, and if I did it correctly, God would reward me. My childhood practice, however innocent, was devoid of the reason to go in secret. The goal shouldn't have been to get a reward, like picking out a toy after finishing up at the dentist's office; that completely misses the point.

---

[2] Dale Bruner, *Matthew: A Commentary Vol. 1 The Christbook*.; Revised & expanded edition (Eerdmans, 2007), 287.
[3] *Book of Common Prayer* (Church Publishing, 1979), 355.

If we're out to get a material reward for our quiet faithfulness, then we'll be sorely disappointed. In this passage, the reward can appear modest: we will receive attention from God. When we go in private to pray, then our heavenly Father notices us—he *sees* us in secret. The reward is as simple as that: God notices us. Jesus doesn't promise riches or fame for praying behind closed doors, rather, we are given something of infinite importance.

As a husband and father, I am learning my family wants my love and attention more than anything else. When I'm playing with my daughter, she wants me to be fully present with her. When I'm talking with my wife, my phone should be on silent, and the TV turned off. If our relationship matters, I'll prove that to my family by the attention I give to them. That's exactly what I wanted from my parents growing up, and they graciously gave their time and attention to me and my brother. I knew they loved me because of the way they acted.

Honestly, it is hard to dote when either party is distracted, and that's partly what prayer is. God pours his adoring attention on us, and we pour out ourselves in honest conversation with him. For the relationship to work, privacy is key. Prayer is not principally a tool for evangelism, it's not meant to inspire others; it is meant to go unnoticed by others, and yet, fully noticed by our Father, who sees in secret.

Reflection: Whose attention do you long to have? What lengths have you gone to get their attention? How might this passage reshape your priorities?

Day 3 • MATTHEW 6:7-8

The ancient pagans had a rule: if you wanted something from the gods, you'd have to wear them down first. The Greek and Roman gods were not at the beck and call of mortals. In fact, they cared little for humans. They were impulsive, destructive, and self-centered. Zeus was a menace when he descended from his throne on Mount Olympus to flirt with (and usually defile) the young women of the earth. There was nothing morally admirable about their qualities. The gods were to be appeased at all costs, and maybe, just maybe, they would send rain in a drought or give their protection during a war.

It was the job of humans to pray constantly and offer sacrifices to ensure the gods' anger did not turn on them. You never knew where you stood with the gods; the only indicator would be the final yield at harvest time, or the safe delivery of a newborn baby. In more extreme cases, priests would have to up the ante to ensure the gods were paying attention. You may remember during the showdown between the prophets of Baal and Elijah on Mount Carmel that the prophets resorted to cutting themselves to get Baal's attention (1 Kings 18:28). Cry out to the gods louder and longer, and if all else fails, shed some blood. Surely, they will notice then.

Jesus' continued teaching on prayer is quite the opposite. Less is more when talking with the One True God. "Empty phrases" are just that: hollow and useless. Our God does not need to be worn down. He is the antithesis of Zeus and Baal in that way. He is present, attentive, and cares for his creation. He is not reluctant to hear what we have to say.

The best advice I've heard on prayer is: "Keep it simple. Keep it honest. Keep it going." [4] I think it is harder for us to distill our prayers into that model than for us to keep rambling on. If we overcomplicate our prayers, or aren't honest in them, then we shouldn't be surprised when we drop the practice all together. We are simply going through the motions, and it benefits no one.

On a trip to Tanzania, I became friends with a local seminary professor. We spent a week driving around the country interviewing local church leaders for a project I was working on. In my time with him, his profound faith in God struck me. I've never met a more prayer-filled person. He constantly talked to God, thanking him for the beauty and wonder around him. He reminded me of how Tevye constantly talks with God in the play *Fiddler on the Roof*. If there was a

[4] Brother Luigi Gioia, Alpha Film Series Ep 5 "Why and How Do I Pray?" (Thomas Nelson, 2016).

lull in our conversation, he would quietly sing a hymn under his breath. When we finished our conversation, he would pick up where he left off with God. It was in no way pretentious or self-serving; it was instead the fruit of a long life dedicated to prayer. He taught me there was a way to "pray without ceasing," as Paul says (1 Thessalonians 5:17), while keeping it simple and honest.

The life of the baptized is a life committed to keeping the conversation going.

Reflection: Is there a prayerful person who has inspired you in your life in Christ? What did you learn from them?

Day 4 • MATTHEW 6:9-15

There is a wonderful homeless ministry in downtown Nashville called Church in the Yard. Every Sunday afternoon, the Church of the Holy Trinity opens its small courtyard to anyone on the streets. The offer is simple: come worship with us, have some lunch, and rest for a while in the shade. It is a beautiful sight to behold.

In the folding chairs around the courtyard is a diverse gathering of people, every race and creed represented, with volunteers interspersed throughout. The altar for the service is a small plastic table with a white linen on it, usually with a Bible on top so the wind doesn't blow the linen away. And then, from around the corner, a priest comes out of the sacristy door wearing his vestments with his blue jeans and boots peeking out of the bottom. Some regulars know the flow of the service, but many do not. They either follow along in the bulletin or sit back and nap while the liturgy is happening. It is foreign for many, even those who grew up in a church environment.

Just when you think a majority of those in the courtyard have mentally checked out, the priest begins the prayer, "Our Father, who art in heaven..." and everyone perks up and recites the prayer with him. The daydreamers, nappers, and even the guys across the street waiting for the food to be served participate in this prayer.

It is a prayer that unites Christians from every country, culture, and language. St. George's Cathedral in Jerusalem has visitors from around the world attend their daily Eucharist, and the priest will introduce the Lord's Prayer by saying, "And now, as our Savior Christ has taught us, we are bold to say in our native tongue..." It then sounds like Pentecost as each person returns to their mother tongue to recite this prayer they learned as a child.

Jesus taught his disciples many things. The Gospels are full of his teachings, but he taught them only one prayer. It appears everything that could or should be said is within in the Lord's Prayer. Countless books have been written on it, every preacher has touched on it, and scholars have dissected it from every angle. But what makes this prayer so profound is its simplicity. Everything Jesus said about prayer in the last few verses is distilled into fifty-seven Greek words. It is accessible enough a child can memorize it and profound enough it has stood the test of time, passed down by each succeeding generation for two millennia. It is the pillar of all Christian prayer; we say this prayer at baptisms, weddings, and even funerals.

But our familiarity with this prayer shouldn't lull us into thinking we automatically know all its implications for us.

We mustn't forget this very "religious" prayer focuses a lot on humans' daily needs. Jesus addresses things like hunger and forgiving debts and trespasses to remind us "Our Father" cares about those things too.

Rowan Williams reminds us there is an earthiness, a groundedness, in our baptismal calling. Baptism doesn't separate us from the world, but links us closer to it. We are washed and cleansed, but also "pushed into the middle of a human situation that will…not leave us untouched or unsullied," he says.[5] This is ultimately what Jesus' incarnation means for us. He is a God who will move into our neighborhood, walk our streets, rub shoulders with us, and embrace our messy human situation.

This is an incarnational prayer, taught by an incarnational God. People have prayed this on city street corners, in beautiful cathedrals, and behind closed doors for two thousand years. If there ever was a baptismal anthem that both inspires the faithful and pushes us to live out our calling, it is this simple prayer.

Reflection: How does the Lord's Prayer inspire you to be more connected to the human messiness surrounding you?

---

[5] Rowan Williams, *Being Christian* (Eerdmans, 2014), 6.

Day 5 • MATTHEW 6:16-18

Intermittent fasting is a diet trend that has become more popular over the past few years. You can try several different approaches: skip breakfast and eat lunch and dinner within an eight-hour window; fast every other day; or with the five-two principle, you diet for five days and fast for two. The fans of this new diet rave about the outcomes.

A buddy of mine recently told me he's started skipping breakfast every morning and can do his work just fine. I wanted to ask him if his coworkers agreed with that statement, especially when he gets hangry around eleven in the morning and snaps at them. But even the Mayo Clinic has seen some positive benefits of it like reducing inflammation which can improve conditions like arthritis and Alzheimer's.[6]

I couldn't help but chuckle when I first heard fasting was the new diet craze. For one thing, it isn't new. And second, I doubt the monks and nuns who regularly fast have ever been interviewed on the health benefits they've received from this practice. I can only imagine one of them saying, "It's not only good for the body, but also the soul."

Fasting is not exclusively a Christian practice, but it has been a part of our discipline from the earliest times of the Church. Though Paul never mentions it, and these three verses are the only ones Jesus directly encourages it, the early Church took on the practice, particularly during seasons of preparation.

It was required for those preparing for baptism, known as catechumens. Depending on the local custom, this preparation process would take one to three years. Fasting was an integral part of the process, especially during Lent, as they drew closer to their baptism on the Easter Vigil. The last thing the soon-to-be Christians thought about while fasting was the inherent medical benefits. It had everything to do with taming their passions, restricting their indulgences, embracing the discomfort, and simplifying one's life. We learn while fasting just how fragile we are and how dependent we are on "our daily bread."

Fasting is yet another way of "practicing our righteousness," as Jesus said. In the same spirit of almsgiving and prayer, we are reminded that spiritual

---

[6] Manpreet Mundi M.D., "What Is Intermittent Fasting? Does it Have Health Benefits?" *Mayo Clinic*, May 5, 2022, https://www.mayoclinic.org/healthy-lifestyle/nutrition-and-healthy-eating/expert-answers/intermittent-fasting/faq-20441303.

disciplines, like fasting, are for God's eyes only. We shouldn't be showy and disfigure our faces so that others can see, nor should we go around telling people what we're up to! The great difference between diet fasting and Jesus-centered fasting is it's not the world's business to know if we're doing it or not.

We could substitute any spiritual discipline for the word "fasting" in this passage.[7] When we go out of our way to be noticed by anyone but God, we completely miss the point. We see for a third time our Father, who sees us acting in secret, will notice us.

If there is anything we have learned over these last few verses, it's the cost of being known to God means being unknown (or unnoticed) by others. The cost is undoubtedly worth it, but it will require we dismiss our pride and let go of our ego.

I believe this is the great lesson the early catechumens were to learn before Easter arrived. They were already building up their spiritual muscles before entering those baptismal waters. For many of us, we have the opposite challenge. We were baptized into the faith and must now learn the great call put on our lives because of our baptism. We have as much unlearning to do as we do learning. This will take time, but thankfully, our God is patient. He simply asks us to keep following and trusting him, as we learn what it truly means to be his disciple.

Reflection: Other than food, what other things in your life do you think would be good to fast from for a time? How does email, social media, or Netflix consume your time and attention?

---

[7] Dale Bruner, *Matthew: A Commentary Vol. 1 The Christbook* (Eerdmans, 2007), 318.

Day 6 • MATTHEW 6:19-21

As I am writing this, my neighbor is getting some major yardwork done. In fact, my neighbor has had numerous projects going for the past six weeks. First, she had the front of her house redone, then she had a new driveway put in, and then a complete remodeling of the flower bed. It now looks like an English garden over there, while just across the street, I'm struggling to keep my grass alive in this Texas heat. I'm happy for her, but I can't help but be a little jealous (okay, maybe really jealous). Keeping up with the Jones' is exhausting, both mentally and financially.

We live in a culture that constantly reminds us we never have enough. The daily bombardment of TV and internet ads beckon us to consume more and more. I just bought a new pair of dress shoes, and all the Facebook ads are now reminding me of every other pair I should've purchased instead. It is a vicious cycle.

So much of how we function in modern society is based on certain insecurities.

According to the Jesuit writer Dean Brackley, we seek security in life through "Upward Mobility."[8] A great example of this is the idea of the American dream. When we talk about the American dream, we usually describe success as getting a college education, buying a home in the suburbs, and driving a nice car.

A common metaphor is "climbing up the ladder," whether in the corporate world or general societal terms. When someone is successful, we use phrases like, "You're moving up in life," or, "You're going somewhere." We not only strive to get our kids into certain types of schools, but we may also be picky about where we buy our groceries and clothes, because these are all indicators of where we are on the social ladder.

Those at the top of the ladder supposedly are the models of society. They serve as an example of what success looks like. Upward mobility can be good, but as Jesus reminds us, it can easily become a god. The desire for success can breed a culture of competition that deems some as winners and others as losers.

We find those deemed outcasts and losers at the bottom of this social ladder—those who have not lived up to "The Dream" or reached certain societal

---

[8] Dean Brackley, "Downward Mobility: Social Implications of St. Ignatius's Two Standards" *Studies in the Spirituality of Jesuits*. Vol. 20. No. 1 (1988).

standards. Society sees them as weak and helpless; they are the image of "downward mobility," according to Brackley.[9]

But according to Jesus, moving down is the only way to truly move up. Or another way of saying it, when you look up (to the Father), going down doesn't seem like a demotion at all. Jesus lived a downwardly mobile life. He was unafraid of how people perceived him, especially with the company he kept. Social status was the last thing on his mind.

That was never more apparent than at Jesus' baptism. He went into the Jordan River, not because he needed it, but so that we could be more like him. He met us on our level, rubbing shoulders with sinners as they received John's baptism of forgiveness. Sinless Jesus, being washed in a baptism he doesn't need, sums up his life, death, and resurrection in this one powerful image. Jesus is always and forever moving down toward us, so that we might move up toward him.

So with that in mind, where do we store our treasures? Are we bent on accruing more in this life, or saving up for the life to come? If we are meant to surrender to Jesus, and trust in his provision, then we must let go of our desire for status and security that a little ole moth can ruin. If that all fails, then simply following G. K. Chesterton's advice may have to suffice, "To be clever enough to get all that money, one must be stupid enough to want it."[10] With Gospel living, downward mobility is the name of the game.

Reflection: What is the most challenging aspect of trusting God to provide for us? What may be the great gift in it?

---

[9] Dean Brackley, "Downward Mobility: Social Implications of St. Ignatius's Two Standards" *Studies in the Spirituality of Jesuits*. Vol. 20. No. 1 (1988).
[10] G.K. Chesterton, *The Innocence of Father Brown* (Warbler Classics, 2021).

Day 7 • MATTHEW 6:1-21

Throughout Matthew 6, Jesus has been giving us some tangible lessons we can put into practice. He has shown us the dos and don'ts of discipleship. Practicing our righteousness has less to do with being flashy and more with the quiet—and sincere—disposition in which we should live out our faith. He is a God of the "secret places," One who desires closed doors and short, honest prayers. And when we don't know what to pray, he has given us one prayer that will more than suffice.

Over the years, the Pharisees added so much to what the Torah had already said. They had heaped interpretations and clarifications so high that you could barely see the commands God originally gave to Moses. In this chapter, Jesus has cleared much of that away. He has simplified it, but not necessarily made it easier for us. He has cut to the core, the very spirit, in which God first gave the Law. It requires that we simplify ourselves and go against the temptation to seek praise and glory.

St. Augustine, the great fifth-century bishop from North Africa, gave some keen advice on this topic. He said, "Emulate the tiny ant; be an ant of God. Listen to the Word of God and hide it in your heart. Collect plenty of food during the happy days of your spiritual summers. You will then be able to endure the difficult days of temptations during the winters of your soul."[11]

We rarely notice ants, yet they continue to do their work quietly and faithfully. Jesus cares not only about our faith, but also about the fruit of that faith. We will live it out one way or another. Being the baptized requires a way of living, and this passage helps us learn the fundamentals. Like a Little League baseball coach teaching the basics of how to catch and throw a ball properly, Jesus is showing us, step-by-step, how to give, pray, forgive, fast, and ultimately how to lay up treasures in heaven. And like a good coach, he knows if we don't consistently practice the fundamentals, then we are liable to create bad habits. If we spend too much time modeling ourselves off the world, or worse, the religious folks who have made it about themselves (the "hypocrites" in Jesus' words), then we too have lost our original calling to be "an ant of God."

What makes Jesus' teaching so challenging is it's so foreign to the way we live today, and it was quite radical, even two thousand years ago. We would say

---

[11] Augustine, "Sermon 38 on the New Testament," *New Advent*, https://www.newadvent.org/fathers/160338.htm Accessed December 12, 2022.

he was turning the world upside down, but I think he understood his work as turning this world right-side up, as N.T. Wright often says in his works.

After all, Adam and Eve's original sin was based on the lie they would be like God. Jesus was teaching his followers what it meant to glorify not oneself but God alone. Shockingly, God doesn't need to be praised on the street corner or with the trumpet sound when giving to the needy. We quickly sense from Jesus that his instruction clarifies how God wants us to live. Matthew 6 shows us the ethic of the kingdom of God, and how God always meant it to be this way, from the Garden of Eden to this very day. This passage isn't meant to simply read; it demands to be lived—for followers of this right-side up kingdom to practice it and take it out into the world

Reflection: What has been the most challenging aspect of this passage? What may God be inviting you into upon further reflection?

week 2
TEMPTATION AND REPENTANCE

Day 8 • MATTHEW 4:1-11

A few years ago, I partnered with a couple of my pastor friends to put on a three-week pub theology event. We thought it would be a great way for our different churches to do something together. While having lunch in a cramped Thai restaurant, the three of us clergy brainstormed the theme of our talks. We quickly realized the easy part was partnering together, but actually nailing down a topic was tricky.

We jokingly said, "How about the seven deadly sins? You know that great medieval list of sins: pride, envy, anger, sloth, covetousness, gluttony, and lust?" But the more we thought about it, the more we were intrigued. Honestly, we were a bit concerned this topic might create a low turnout for the event. Who wants to go to a bar, grab a beer, and then spend an hour talking about deadly sins?

We went through with it not because of the crowds it would bring, or better yet, the crowds we'd possibly scare away, but because of the importance of the topic. We felt we had to do it because we simply don't talk about sin that much, especially in the Episcopal Church.

We rebranded a bit, and entitled the series, "The Seven Sexy Passions." Nothing like adding a little intrigue to grab people's attention. But we also had an actual reason for naming it that. There is something appealing about sins. They call to us, some more than others, but either way, they can be tempting or desirable, or dare I say sexy?

Someone I consider one of the greatest American philosophers of all time, Mark Twain, said, "There is a charm about the forbidden that makes it unspeakably desirable."[12] So, whether you call them sins or passions, they are attractive to us, call our name, know our weakness, and can easily lead us astray. We wouldn't sin unless we enjoyed doing it.

Sin is charming and even desirable because, even though we know it is not good for us, we still do it. Even if we playfully call them the "Sexy Passions," we must not forget the seriousness of sin.

---

[12] Stephen Brennan, *Mark Twain on Common Sense: Timeless Advice and Words of Wisdom from America's Most-Revered Humorist* (Skyhorse, 2014).

There is a reason the medieval theologians called them *deadly* sins. Sin is the one thing that separates us from God. It is the barrier between the fallen creation and the perfect Creator. We are in this mess because we continue to get stuck in the same old ruts of pride, envy, anger, sloth, covetousness, gluttony, and lust. Unfortunately, we must confront these temptations daily.

It should be no surprise in our baptismal service, the priest asks the candidate(s)for Holy Baptism, "Do you renounce Satan and all the spiritual forces of wickedness that rebel against God? Do you renounce the evil powers of this world which corrupt and destroy the creatures of God? Do you renounce all sinful desires that draw you from the love of God?" And each time the candidate says, "I renounce them."[13]

At the very beginning of this new life in Christ, there is an exorcism of sorts. We are forced to name the evil of this world, recognize its existence and influence on us, and turn from it. The one or those being baptized say they will not allow the powers of sin, death, and the devil to create a wedge that will split them from God.

Let's be clear: the Bible and the service for Holy Baptism don't make an argument for the devil's existence. Rather, it not only assumes his existence, but also that he is actively trying to draw us away from God with the same old vices that have plagued humanity from the beginning.

So, call them sexy passions or deadly sins, call them what you want. They continue to split us from the love of God, and only by the power of God can we conquer them.

Reflection: What draws you personally away from God's love? How might you address it?

---

[13] *Book of Common Prayer*, (Church Publishing, 1979), 302.

Day 9 • MATTHEW 4:1

Last week we looked broadly at the Lord's Prayer. In it, Jesus teaches us to pray, "Lead us not into temptation." A way of understanding that petition is we shouldn't come under the influence and power of temptation as Dale Bruner tells us.[14] With that in mind, it's quite ironic that in our passage for today, the Spirit whisks Jesus away—to be tempted. The very thing we earnestly ask God to protect us from ends up happening to Jesus. It appears we can confidently pray this portion of the Lord's Prayer because Jesus was led into temptation so that you and I wouldn't have to be.

For all the places this temptation could happen, all the arenas where Jesus and the devil could duke it out, it is fitting they meet in the wilderness. For the biblical writers, the wilderness was a place of testing. The most well-known example is the Israelites, who spent forty long years in the wilderness. In that time, the generation who disobeyed God at the beginning of their wandering died. It was a time for Israel to unlearn Egypt's ways and discover what it meant to be the people of God before entering the Promised Land.

Later, prophets like Elijah spent time in the wilderness, and Isaiah foretells of a voice that will ring out, "In the wilderness prepare the way of the LORD; make straight in the desert a highway for our God" (Isaiah 40:3b). The wilderness had always had a particular function in the biblical imagination. Yes, it was a place of testing, but it was also a place of renewal. Something good can come out of such a lifeless place. Even in a landscape that claims so much death, God can bring forth life. Ezekiel's vision of a valley of dry bones that comes to life is a great example of this (Ezekiel 37).

The particular wilderness church tradition tells us Jesus was sent to is not very far from the Jordan River, where he had just received his baptism by John. It is a dry and barren place with no trees in sight. But that doesn't mean it was *nowhere*, completely away from everything else. If you find yourself on the top of the Mount of Olives in Jerusalem, you can look to the west and see the hustle and bustle of the Holy City. If you look to the east, you'll see the very wilderness where we believe Satan tempted Jesus. The temptations take place just out of the reach of both Jerusalem and the Jordan. Away from the religious piety of the Temple, and still dripping in the waters of his baptism, Jesus is straddling the line between these two worlds. The world as it is (i.e., Jerusalem), and the new movement God is bringing about (i.e., John's baptism).

[14] Dale Bruner, Matthew: *A Commentary Volume 1 Revised ed* (Eerdmans, 2007), 312–313.

Over the next few days, we'll consider the particularities of temptation, but we mustn't forget that *place* inherently matters. It meant a great deal to the biblical writers, so we should also take heed of its importance. Our temptations may take place primarily within ourselves, in our hearts and minds, but we must reckon with the physical nature of it as well. Being tempted is not just a spiritual battle but also challenges the body; a body that inhabits space and time. Our wilderness may look very different from Jesus', but it is also between the world as is, and the new thing God wants to bring about in us. When we find ourselves in temptation's hour, God promises us we will not be in that place alone. We can lean on our Lord for strength and guidance because he has already gone before us and created a highway out of the wilderness of temptation and into his grace and freedom.

Reflection: What does the wilderness look like for you? How have you dealt with those moments of isolation and temptation in your life?

Day 10 • MATTHEW 4:2-4

Between 1527 and 1529, Martin Luther penned some of the most memorable stanzas in Christian hymnody. This project culminated in what we know as, "A Mighty Fortress is Our God." Most of this classic hymn was based on Psalm 46, but Luther also infused his personal experiences into it. He was a passionate reformer who ushered in a new era in the church's history, but his miserable offenses plagued him in light of a perfect and holy God. Paul's letter to the Romans would help him sort some of this out.

Luther knew this was not just his personal battle with sin, but a cosmic battle between good and evil, light and darkness. His masterful hymn names the darkness like few other Christian songs ever have.[15]

"For still our ancient foe
doth seek to work us woe;
his craft and power are great,
and armed with cruel hate,
on earth is not his equal."
(Verse 1)

It then continues,
"The prince of darkness grim,
we tremble not for him;
his rage we can endure,
for lo! his doom is sure;
one little word shall fell him."
(Verse 3)

I believe Luther clears a path for preachers and teachers to begin to talk about the devil, the tempter, or as Jesus said in the Lord's Prayer, "the evil one." Luther both acknowledges his existence, while also recognizing his power is limited. One small word will ruin him, after all.

We either come out of a tradition that talked too much about the devil or too little. I've never met anyone who said there was just the right amount of devil-talk from their pulpit.

---

[15] *The Hymnal* (Church Publishing, 1982), 688.

Fleming Rutledge has been a helpful voice within my tradition to clarify what the devil is and isn't. She reminds us we use the term, "devil" to personify the cosmic power of evil. We can say with confidence there is a malignant force out in the universe working to undo God's good creation. This force does all in its power to unravel what God has put together.[16] Whether you believe in a Satan that has two horns, a tail, and pitchfork is really not that interesting from a theological perspective. There is so much more going on than that simple idea of evil.

Paul the Apostle talks about the cosmic powers of evil concerning sin, death, and the devil. We typically spend too much time in the church obsessing over the latter that we never see the triumvirate as a collective unit.[17]

One great trap we fall into is the notion the devil is on equal footing with God. Though evil is God's enemy, it is neither omnipotent nor omnipresent. My college New Testament professor liked to say, "If the devil is after you, then I'm relieved because that means he's not after me" (Dr. Roger Green, Gordon College)! The devil is powerful, but we should never dare think he is God's equal.

The true power the wields is the art of persuasion. His name in Greek, *diabolos*, can be traced to the verb that means "to split." From Genesis 3 onward, he does a great job of splitting us from God. Shockingly in our passage, he uses Scripture to persuade Jesus to eat. The devil knows the Bible and shrewdly twists its words for his own benefit.

If we learn anything from this passage, it's that we know evil's game plan against us. These cosmic powers of darkness meet us in our weakness and offer the very thing we desire. Note how the tempter promises bread to hungry Jesus. He comes to us when we are alone, at our wit's end, and most especially, when we're doubting ourselves (and God). But the great *Undo-er* is not the Almighty God. We need not be enslaved to him, nor put up with his schemes. We must call out to Jesus. For as Luther said, it is this little word that "shall fell him."

Reflection: What is tempting you these days? How might this understanding of evil's limitations help you move forward in your life in Christ?

---

[16] Fleming Rutledge, *The Crucifixion: Understanding the Death of Jesus Christ* reprint (Eerdmans, 2017), 437.
[17] Fleming Rutledge, *The Crucifixion: Understanding the Death of Jesus Christ* reprint (Eerdmans, 2017), Chapter 9.

Day 11 • MATTHEW 4:5-7

In most job interviews, there comes a time when the interviewer asks you to describe your strengths and weaknesses. I don't know about you, but I have a long list of strengths I can conjure up on why I'd be a good fit for the job. I guess it's the salesman in me, but more likely, it's my ego. Undoubtedly, I have many weaknesses as well, but I'm much more reticent to share those.

I've been on the other side of the interview table when the applicant either can't think of a weakness they have, or they name one, which then leads them to talk about another one of their strengths. I have to say, since I've been married, I'm much more aware of my faults and weaknesses. My wife would tell you the list is growing by the day.

The tempter perceived Jesus' strengths and weaknesses as well. He first went after Jesus' hunger. It had been forty long days of fasting, and there was nothing more Jesus wanted physically than food. "Simply say the words," the devil says, "and the stones in front of you can become freshly baked bread." But Jesus rebuffs the temptation with a line from Deuteronomy 8:3.

They then move from the barren wilderness to the holiest place on Earth. It is on top of the Temple that the devil makes his next move in this wicked game of chess. This time, he changes his approach by going after Jesus' strength. "You know the Bible," he says, "so jump and you'll be taken care of. You won't even have a scratch." He tries to lull him into sinning by taking him to a familiar place and then quoting Scripture to him.

It must have been a strange feeling for Jesus. Looking down from that great height in Jerusalem, he could recall when, as a teenager, he told his mother she could always find him in his Father's house. Under those porticoes, he sat and watched the faithful pour into the outer courtyard during all the major festivals throughout the years. And now he's standing with the great enemy of God, and is being quoted Scripture, the very Scripture he inspired the biblical authors to write!

With each temptation, the devil is progressively trying to sow seeds of doubt in Jesus' mind. Doubt of his divine call at baptism when he heard his heavenly Father say, "This is my beloved Son, whom I love; with him I am well pleased" (Matthew 3:17 NIV). But also doubt of God's faithfulness and protection. Will God actually not allow his foot to dash a stone?

This teaches us an important lesson. Temptation comes not only in our lowest moments, but even at the pinnacle of life. When things seem to go well, when we are comfortable in a familiar place, that is when sin can slyly wrap around us. It may even take the things we are most confident in and use them against us.

How many times have we seen athletes, politicians, and even pastors fall from grace when they are at their "peak"? Financial and sexual sins are so prominent when someone has gotten comfortable with their success. The devil's presence around the Temple should be a warning, especially for those of us churchgoers. He seemed quite comfortable bringing Jesus to that sacred place. Evil, the great Un-Doer of God's good creation, will not hesitate to infiltrate our places of worship if we allow it, and will gladly misconstrue the words of the Bible for his benefit.

Jesus conquers this second temptation through faithful exegesis of Scripture, and the unflinching belief that God meant what he said at his baptism. No test was needed. When God said he loved him and was well pleased, Jesus believed him.

This should be an encouragement for us. The baptized are called to a life of belief. Believe God's promises are worth your trust. He is faithful. When we welcome the newly baptized into the household of God, and seal them as Christ's own forever, our only requirement is to believe it is true. God has made us his own, and he will not forsake us. Even in temptation's hour, he is there offering another way.

Reflection: What have moments of weakness and doubt taught you about yourself? What have they taught you about God?

Day 12 • MATTHEW 4:8-10

When someone asks me when I felt a call to ministry, I normally begin with a story from my childhood. I grew up in a churchgoing family. It was not as much of a command as a routine or habit. Something would've felt off about the week if we didn't go to church on Sunday.

We usually sat in one of the small transepts just off from the altar. Thinking about it now, my mother probably chose that spot so that we could exit quickly if I got fussy. But more times than not, as a three- or four-year-old, I would sit under the pew, munch on Cheerios, and listen to the service. I took it all in: the beautiful hymns, the rhythmic prayers, and the sermon that seemed to always make people laugh at the beginning and turn serious by the end. For the climactic moment of the service, we would make our way to the altar for communion. Later in life, I realized I fell in love with the worship of God before knowing anything about him. The rituals and liturgies in that small Episcopal church shaped my imagination of who this God must be. The way we worshiped inherently reflected our beliefs in this God.

Writers like David Foster Wallace and singers like Bob Dylan knew all too well that we must worship (i.e. serve) something or someone.

Wallace said, "There is no thing as not worshiping. Everybody worships. The only choice we get is what to worship."[18] And Dylan's classic song "Gotta Serve Somebody," makes a similar point.

These two men used their artistic medium to challenge us to reflect on what we truly worship. There is something deep in our soul that pushes us to worship that which is bigger than ourselves. When we encounter something majestic and awe-inspiring, we can't help but fall to our knees.

God created us to worship.

It is then so interesting the devil tries to lure Jesus to worship him. Through this temptation narrative, we have been progressively moving skyward. We began in the wilderness, moved up to the pinnacle of the Temple, and now we find them on top of a mountain. The higher they've gone up, the bigger the requests have become. What began with a seemingly innocent challenge to

---

[18] David Foster Wallace, *This is Water: Some Thoughts, Delivered on a Significant Occasion, about Living a Compassionate Life* (Little Brown and Company, 2009).

change stones into bread has now escalated to displaying the kingdoms of the world in hopes of being worshiped.

As the master of lies, the tempter has yet again manipulated the truth. It is not his right to give away the kingdoms of the world, they're not his to begin with. He may have methods for sowing sin into the great powers of the world, but surely, he doesn't possess them. If this world has been the devil's playground, then through these temptations, Jesus is showing us he is taking back what is rightfully his.

The Apostle Paul reminds us Jesus didn't take what was rightfully his through sheer force. He did not appear with the heavenly hosts flanking him at his incarnation. Rather, he came humbly, emptying himself of all the rights and privileges of royalty, to be born by lowly Mary.

As these temptations have been moving upward, Jesus has been consistently moving downward. Because of this, Paul claims, "God has highly exalted him and bestowed on him the name that is above every name, so that at the name of Jesus every knee should bow, in heaven and on earth and under the earth, and every tongue confess that Jesus Christ is Lord, to the glory of God the Father" (Philippians 2:9–11).

True worship belongs not to the tempter who is the king of lies, but to the Humble One, the Crucified and Resurrected One.

Reflection: Bob Dylan's song "Gotta Serve Somebody" reminds us that no matter who we are, we have to serve someone. What are some things you worship? What does that say about what you value?

Day 13 • MATTHEW 4:11

Like a boxer who has survived round after punishing round, Jesus is exhausted. He has won this fight, but he must get stitched up before making his next move. Along with the verse in John 11 that tells us Jesus wept, I believe the ending of the temptations shows us a profound glimpse into Jesus' humanity. We must not forget Jesus was *fully* human, along with being fully divine. This one line gives us a glimpse of the physical and spiritual toll this took on our Lord. The writer Matthew could have easily not included this line, but for some reason, he wanted us to see Jesus being cared for by the angels. We are reminded that all of heaven must have been transfixed on Jesus' responses to the devil. Jesus had the freedom to give in, and he could've chosen to fall for the tempter's trickery. All of salvation history hinged on Jesus' responses. If that wasn't the case, then the temptations were a formality that simply needed to be checked off.

But everything in our passage points to the freedom Jesus had to say yes or no. With each rebuff of the devil, Jesus' strength and fortitude were tested to their limit. And from that, we can glean Jesus was tempted in every way we are. In our highest and lowest moments, in our strengths and weaknesses, temptation creeps in. If this happened to Jesus, of all people, it would undoubtedly happen to us. We should not be surprised when temptation and trouble come our way.

Many of us unconsciously make a deal with God when we come to faith, are baptized, or try to start "living a better life." As a reward for our faithfulness, we assume God will protect us from all harm. We expect for our loved ones to stay healthy and for our needs to be met. Being a "good Christian" will lead to a generally happy life, many of us assume.

One of my seminary professors, Reverend Dr. Frank Wade, who was a parish priest for years, encountered this way of thinking all the time with his parishioners. He would tell them something like, "You may have signed that deal, but look again because God didn't." Though God hadn't signed a deal for them to live a perfectly happy life, he would tell them, as he would say to us, God promises to be with, guide, and give them strength through the challenges of life to all who call on his name.

Baptism is not a protective bubble; we must look to Jesus. These temptations happen directly after his baptism. He is thrown into the deep end at the beginning of his ministry. Jesus is setting the tone for what was to come over the next three years of his life: he is *with* us, fully and completely. He will not shy away from the Jordan's dirty water, nor the tough challenges of temptation. If Jesus suffered not only hardship but also violence and even an unjust death, then we shouldn't be surprised when we encounter the same. He promises we will not be alone. God himself has dealt with everything we are experiencing. He is faithful, and he calls us to faithfully trust him.

Jesus is known as the second Adam. In the ways the first Adam failed to live an obedient life to God, so this second Adam was obedient, even to the point of death. The first Adam fell from God's grace and was banished from paradise, but this second Adam has assured us we will be with him in paradise. Through Jesus' faith and perfect obedience, he has restored the bridge between God and humanity. We must remember our faith is a gift from God to us. It is this divine faith that inspires us to respond in like manner and live as representatives of this second Adam.

From the temptations to the cross, the Gospels focus us on one thing: God's action for us.

Reflection: Have you made a deal with God and been frustrated with the outcome? Upon further reflection, were you able to see God's faithfulness in that situation?

Day 14 • MATTHEW 4:1-11

Whoever said a boring sermon couldn't lead to something great?

The year was 1940. It was July in England, which meant every window in the church was open to let in the cool breeze. The priest had worked hard on his sermon, knowing the tough crowd that usually sat in the pews on Sunday mornings. Unfortunately for him, his message wasn't cutting it. Many parishioners' minds had begun to wander.

One of the poor souls daydreaming in his pew was C. S. Lewis, one of the great Christian writers of the twentieth century. While the priest methodically made each of his points, Lewis thought of his next writing project. He said, "I was struck by an idea for a book which I think might be both useful and entertaining. It would be called *As One Devil to Another* and would consist of letters from an elderly retired devil to a young devil who has just started work on his first 'patient.'"[19]

It was later renamed *The Screwtape Letters*. In it, a retired devil named Screwtape advises his young nephew on how to lead astray the man he has been assigned to tempt. Slowly but surely, they try to lead the man away from their arch-Enemy: God.

Much of their job is to shape the man's desires away from their heavenly Enemy. It is an insightful book on temptation, in part, because of the subtlety of it all. Like wet clay that needs to be formed, the man in the story is being shaped by good and evil, but in the end, his choices will lead him to be shaped by one more than the other.

At one point, the elder devil says, "It does not matter how small the sins are provided that their cumulative effect is to edge the man away from the Light and out into the nothing. Murder is no better than cards if cards can do the trick. Indeed the safest road to Hell is the gradual one—the gentle slope, soft underfoot, without sudden turnings, without milestones, without signposts."[20]

And so, we end this week where we started. There is something desirable about sin, or we wouldn't participate in it. We are lured by its promises of fulfillment

---

[19] Alister McGrath, C.S. Lewis—*A Life: Eccentric Genius, Reluctant Prophet* (Tyndale Elevate, 2016), 215.Delivered on a Significant Occasion, about Living a Compassionate Life (Little Brown and Company, 2009).
[20] C.S. Lewis, "Letter XII" from the *Screwtape Letters* in *The Complete C.S. Lewis Signature Classics* (Harper Collins, 2002).

and happiness, only to be kicked to the curb in a pile of our own shame and disgrace. There is the fleeting delight of this world, but God has offered us another way: the delight of the kingdom. Both are persuasive in their own ways, but only one will satisfy our true hopes and longings.

We are made for the bread that endures and not mere stones. We are made for the Word that brings life and not lies. We are made for worship that we direct toward what is eternal and holy rather than the crumbling kingdoms of this age. Standing above all this as victor and Savior is none other than the Lord Jesus. It was on a mountain where he conquered the third temptation, it was on the mount of Calvary he conquered death on a cross, and it was a mountain in Galilee where he gathered his disciples one last time and said, "All authority in heaven and earth has been given to me" (Matthew 28:18). He claimed what was rightfully his, not by giving into the devil's schemes, but through faithful obedience to God, even if that obedience ultimately led to suffering and death. We need not drown in our sin and shame. Jesus has thrown us a life jacket, and we claim it in the waters of our baptism. It is by his righteousness that we are made righteous; in his death and resurrection, we are brought into new life.

As Jesus has shown us, temptation doesn't always have to lead to defeat. With him, we can be called into deeper faithfulness—a faith that can endure even the greatest temptations.

Reflection: After reflecting this week, what might you turn over to God? How might you trust his faithfulness and goodness even more in the days ahead?

week 3
BE BORN AGAIN

Day 15 • JOHN 3:1-3

Not too long ago, I went with a friend to a Greek Orthodox vespers service. We entered the church five minutes before the evening prayers began and were surprised the hallway lights weren't on. As we walked into the dimly lit church, there were no greeters, no bulletins, or instructions about what we had just gotten ourselves into. We sat down in silence, and after a few minutes, a couple of priests and cantors appeared from a side door, and then the service promptly began. Most of it was in Greek, as they chanted long portions of ancient prayers and the Psalms. The congregation stood the entire time, which would've been fine if the service didn't last for two and a half hours!

It was a beautiful service, even though I couldn't feel my feet by the end of it. As my buddy and I limped back to our cars, we were struck by the lack of hospitality. What if we were looking for a church? They made no effort to get our info or tell us their mission statement. They didn't even take up a collection. Who does that?

On the other hand, the way they do church is quite refreshing. Most congregations have tried to be seeker-friendly. You may be greeted by someone at the door, but more likely, you'll be mauled by eight different volunteers, each of whom will ask for your email address and phone number. We play popular easy-to-listen-to hymns. We have creative sermon series that will go deep but not too deep to avoid offending. For some parishes, catering to the unknown seeker in our midst has made us water down the whole business to which the church is called. We have made it more about the seekers than we have about God. This Greek Orthodox church may lack a sophisticated welcome committee, but they are a great reminder church is first and foremost about the worship of God.

It would be fair to say Nicodemus was a seeker. He comes to Jesus under the cover of darkness for a personal Q&A session. Talking at this hour of the night will allow him to hear from the popular rabbi without being disturbed by others, but it will also ensure his fellow Pharisees are ignorant of his whereabouts. They are suspicious of this Nazarene teacher, but Nicodemus is a semi-believer, gathering more details about Jesus. He believes he can gain more from talking to Jesus than the social standing he might lose. Jesus welcomes the conversation, but he doesn't make it easy. He challenges and pushes this seeker to come to a fuller understanding of what God is up to. Nicodemus recognizes him as a teacher, but Jesus is trying to show him that he is much more. Jesus is bent on Nicodemus' full conversion, so he can walk out of the darkness and into the light.

Coddling seekers may not be the church's best approach. A real, honest conversation about the things that matter—the eternal things—may be a better approach.

Believe it or not, we have many spiritual seekers in our pews every week. They are the teenagers sitting in our congregations. If my youth ministry days taught me anything, it's that teenagers long for authentic relationships and straightforward conversations. So much of their lives are determined by others that they jump in completely when they have the opportunity for something real (something actually theirs). They will ask some of the deepest questions, and you better believe they will sense if you're lying.

Like Nicodemus, they are hungry to know more; they want to know Jesus, and it's our responsibility to show them the real Jesus. We've lost so many young people in the church because we have stuck with the same clichés we taught them in Vacation Bible School. It never went any deeper than that. Jesus didn't dumb things down for the seeker who came to him that night, and it's best if we don't do it with those in our pews, either. Nicodemus is both outside and inside our churches, and how we respond to him is our choice. Over this week, we'll see the deep, lasting life Jesus offers each of us—seekers and experts—and the challenging call he places on all of us to be born again.

Reflection: Have you ever felt like a seeker or know someone who would identify as one? What is it we all seek deep down?

Day 16 • JOHN 3:4

A certain amount of snobbery can run through some academic circles (note I didn't say all). Knowledge is power, and it's hard to argue with someone who has dedicated themselves to a life of study. The New Atheists—a group led by well-respected thinkers like Sam Harris, Richard Dawkins, and Christopher Hitchens—have made it their mission to show how outrageous it is to believe in God. Not only is theism laughable, but the evil done by religion is unforgivable. More often than not, they will talk about the simple-mindedness of the first-century peasants who followed Jesus. The ancients lived in a magical world where demons ran around freely, virgins gave birth to children, and people rose from the dead. Us modern folks have wised up, they claim. Thanks to the Enlightenment, we won't be fooled by fanciful thinking any longer.

Nicodemus was no modern scientist, yet he had trouble squaring what Jesus said and what he knew about biology. "How does this born again thing work? How can someone who is old enter their mother's womb?" You didn't need a degree from Oxford to know birth doesn't work that way.

Nicodemus was not the first of his kind. The question of "how" continued to come up when God was doing something new in the world. When the angel told Zechariah he and Elizabeth would have a son in their old age, the first thing out of his mouth was, "How shall I know this" (Luke 1:18)? When Mary was told she would give birth to the Savior, she asked, "How will this be, since I am a virgin" (Luke 1:34)? Even Thomas, at the news of his Lord's resurrection, knew dead men don't just get up and walk again. He wanted to see the proof and physically touch the scars.

These people were anything but simple. What God was up to was simply that radical.

The irony in Nicodemus' question only comes to light when we first look at how he addressed Jesus in verse 2. He says, "Jesus, we know you come from God because of all the great signs and wonders you do." If Nicodemus is confident Jesus is from God, and the Hebrew Scriptures say God can do anything, then why is being born again so difficult to comprehend? Has he forgotten the plagues in Egypt? What about crossing the Red Sea, the manna from heaven, or the chariots of fire? Being born again seems like a cakewalk compared to some of these other events.

No doubt Nicodemus asks a good question. I would've asked Jesus, but we must also realize who we are dealing with. If this is, in fact, the God who created everything out of nothing (ex nihilo), then all bets are off. The God of all creation has no limitations.

Nicodemus must learn this important lesson before understanding what Jesus really means about the new birth. *How* and *why* are good, honest questions, but sometimes you must realize who you're talking to. If Nicodemus hasn't learned it yet, he will very soon.

Reflection: What limitations have you put on God? Has he surprised you when he extended the boundaries you put on him?

Day 17 • JOHN 3:5-6

The second-century Church Father Tertullian once said, "Christians are made, not born."[21] No one has the right to claim the Christian faith as a birthright. God only has children, not grandchildren, as Will Willimon likes to say.[22] As Jesus put it, "That which is born of the flesh is flesh, and that which is born of Spirit is spirit" (John 3:6). Even if you are born to Christian parents, you must enter the waters of baptism yourself. Each of us is called to be remade and recreated through this sacrament of new birth.

The work of baptism is the work of the Holy Spirit. We call on the Holy Spirit to bless the baptismal waters and recall all the ways he has already moved through that life-giving substance. He hovered over the watery chaos in creation. He went through it as he led Israel through the Red Sea and in it when Jesus was baptized.[23]

But the baptism Jesus instituted differed greatly from what John was doing at the Jordan River. Judaism had a ritual washing that would ensure someone would not be "unclean" forever (i.e., Leviticus 17:15). They would wash in a ritual bath known as a "mikvah." A person would walk down the steps of the mikvah unclean, go through the waters, and then walk up the other side clean in the eyes of the Torah. John the Baptist simply goes to the banks of the Jordan and makes the whole river his mikvah. Instead of washing to be clean and return to normal life, John is washing an entire nation to prepare for the Messiah. His baptism is charged with the expectation of God's imminent arrival.

Where John's was a baptism of forgiveness and anticipation, Jesus' was of new birth. His requires water and the Spirit. To be "born again" suggested not what you had to do but what you had to become. Calvin understood it to mean we received an entirely new origin, this time "from above."[24] By the grace of our baptism, we are welcomed into God's family. As in a mikvah, we come out of those waters different than we went in, but we receive not only forgiveness but also a family.

---

[21] Tertullian, "Apology," Chapter 18 *New Advent*, https://www.newadvent.org/fathers/0301.htm Accessed December 12, 2022.
[22] Will Willimon in *Remember Who You Are* (Nashville: Upper Room, 1980), p. 22.
[23] *Book of Common Prayer* (Church Publishing, 1979), 306.
[24] "Of Baptism," *Calvin's Institutes*, https://www.ccel.org/ccel/calvin/institutes.vi.xvi.html Accessed December 7, 2022.

In the Episcopal liturgy, after the baptism, the congregation welcomes the newly baptized by saying, "We receive you into the household of God. Confess the faith of Christ crucified, proclaim his resurrection, and share with us in his eternal priesthood."[25]

A friend recently told me of a time she witnessed two young brothers being baptized at the church. They came from a broken family, and only one relative showed up to support them along with their mother. The rest of the family didn't come.

At the point in the service when the congregation welcomed the boys into God's household, they wept. They were now part of a big, beautiful family who loved them and took vows to care for them. New birth for these two boys meant new siblings and more spiritual aunts and uncles than they could ever count. They were finally home.

No matter where we've come from or what we have done, a new birth is waiting for us in those baptismal waters. What appears on the outside to be a few prayers and sprinkling (or submerging) a person in water is the gift of a new origin story.

Paul and the early church fathers said baptism is both our tomb and mother (referring to St. Gregory of Nyssa). In it, we died with Christ and are reborn. This is not a gift for the holy or righteous but for all people from every language, culture, and nation. It is a gift freely given through water and the Spirit.

Reflection: What has the term "born again" meant to you? What is it like to be welcomed into God's family through baptism?

---

[25] *Book of Common Prayer* (Church Publications, 1979), 308.

Day 18 • JOHN 3:7-8

Did Nicodemus give Jesus a look? Was his face turning red, or had his jaw hit the floor? Jesus tells Nicodemus not to be shocked at what he's saying. This is actually what God is up to! Being a son of Abraham (and even a teacher of the Law) are not the credentials that equate to new birth, according to Jesus. Even Nicodemus, with his family lineage (and all his degrees), cannot opt out of this masterclass on God's new action.

Jesus seems to care little about the memberships we hold. We may be members of social or sports clubs, the school board, or a well-respected family, but Jesus shrugs at those status symbols. Even being a member of the local synagogue or church doesn't seem to impress Jesus automatically. Membership in the family of God requires the Spirit's involvement. And if there is anything we know about the Holy Spirit, he goes where he pleases. As elusive as he is, the fruits of his labor are always evident.

We have already referenced the Spirit's involvement in the moment of baptism, but the Spirit's work is not done when the baptismal service ends. The internal work really begins, or better yet, is put into a whole new gear. N. T. Wright considers the Spirit baptism as "the new life, bubbling up from within."[26] It requires an openness on our part for the Holy Spirit to form and shape us. In this scenario, we are not the painter but the canvas; we are not the potter but the clay. Surrendering to this mysterious force is daunting. It will inevitably lead us in ways we may have never intended. But as we say in the Nicene Creed, we believe the Holy Spirit to be "the Lord and giver of life."[27] He graciously gives us new, abundant life on his terms, not ours. Letting go of our need to control is all a part of opening our hands (and hearts) to what the Spirit has for us.

Nicodemus shouldn't have been that surprised by Jesus' words. God had been telling the people of Israel he would do this for a long time. Ezekiel prophesied:

> I will sprinkle clean water on you, and you shall be clean from all your uncleannesses, and from all your idols I will cleanse you. And I will give you a new heart, and a new spirit I will put within you. And I will remove the heart of stone from your flesh and give you a heart of flesh. And I will put my Spirit within you, and cause you to walk in my statutes and be careful to obey my rules. (36:25–27)

---

[26] N.T. Wright, *John for Everyone, Part 1* (Westminster: John Knox Press, 2004), 30.
[27] *Book of Common Prayer* (Church Publications, 1979), 359.

The nighttime *seeker* has now become the *discoverer*. Through this conversation with Jesus, Nicodemus realizes this prophecy will be fulfilled in his lifetime by the man standing before him. The Spirit is doing a new thing, and he is starting with Nicodemus. An honest inquiry has quickly turned into a full-on revelation of God's plan for salvation.

And maybe the lesson for us is a little curiosity will go a long way with the Holy Spirit. Just coming to ask a question may open the door for the Spirit to move and shape us; for his presence to "bubble up" within us. The goal, then, is not to take ourselves too seriously, especially the titles we may hold. God is not looking at all the different memberships we possess but at the inquiring spirit within us.

Reflection: What do you discern the Lord is bubbling up in your life today? How might God use your curiosity for his glory?

Day 19 • JOHN 3:9-13

I'm very aware as a priest that the group Jesus personally challenges constantly is the religious elite. The teachers and leaders of Israel continue to be a roadblock to Jesus' work and a constant nagging presence in his ministry. They are offended that he will not conform to their standards. He eats with sinners and outcasts, does wondrous miracles on the Sabbath, and teaches with an otherworldly authority. Jesus has neither asked for their blessing to do these things nor sought to play their political games.

"Are you the teacher of Israel and yet you do not understand these things?" (John 3:10)

Today, there is little trust in institutions, whether the government, universities, or the church. Scandal and wholesale corruption have weakened the overall voice of these traditional places of power. A 2021 article by the United Nations stated Americans' trust in the national government declined from 73 percent in 1958 to a meager 24 percent in 2021.[28] The church in the West has steadily been losing members, and the COVID-19 pandemic only expedited the process. Even those who have stayed in the parish wisely are not keen on blindly trusting their superiors.

An extreme example is a woman I was talking to at lunch in seminary one day. She was about to be ordained but then went on a rant about her bishop. She said, "I don't care what he says. I don't have to listen to him." The irony is she needed that bishop to be ordained. During the ordination service, she would have to promise to obey her bishop. I'm assuming she crossed her fingers during that part of the service.

But I don't think it has to be either extreme. Institutions are broken because broken people fill them. When there is sin and corruption, we should deal with it rather than push it under the rug. Institutions do not have it in their nature to change, or at least not to change quickly. It is not a bad thing for there to be a prophetic voice from within the institution that calls it to be better and live into its ideals.

---

[28] "Trust in Public Institutions: Trends and Implications for Economic Security," *United Nations Department of Economic and Social Affairs*, July 20, 2021. https://www.un.org/development/desa/dspd/2021/07/trust-public-institutions/

Abraham Lincoln embodied this so well throughout his presidency. He spoke directly to this in his first inaugural address when he said, "We are not enemies, but friends. We must not be enemies. Though passion may have strained, it must not break our bonds of affection. The mystic chords of memory will swell when again touched, as surely they will be, by the better angels of our nature."[29] He was confident the Union (the institution of government) must continue to stand amid chaos and open rebellion. He didn't say this as a command to the citizens of this country but *as a fellow citizen*. He was within their ranks, calling them to seek the good of the collective whole.

Jesus speaks within the Jewish community as a Jew. He pushes Nicodemus to recognize his ignorance and the blindness of the religious elite, but Jesus doesn't leave him hanging for long. He cannot get into heavenly things because Nicodemus cannot handle earthly things. He must know now heaven has descended with the Son of Man. The Answer is standing right in front of Nicodemus.

We learn Jesus was not trying to destroy the institution Nicodemus represented but to fill it with his truth from the inside out. Nicodemus might be an agent for Jesus within the halls of power in Jerusalem. It's not only individuals who need to discern the Spirit's movement, but communities and institutions should also do it. It may even be more radical to consider God is transforming from within rather than without.

Reflection: How might God be working in the institutions around us? How might God be calling us to be his agents within those institutions like Nicodemus?

---

[29] Abraham Lincoln, "First Inaugural of Address of Abraham Lincoln," *Yale Law School – Lillian Goldman Law Library*, https://avalon.law.yale.edu/19th_century/lincoln1.asp Accessed December 14, 2022.

Day 20 • JOHN 3:14-15

I hate snakes. I don't want to see them, touch them, or even think about them. I read a book not too long ago about snake-handling churches in Appalachia called *Salvation on Sand Mountain*. The front cover has a man holding a huge snake, so I put sticky notes all over the front of the book. I could read about them, but I still didn't want to see them.

It is odd to me that snakes have made their way into Christian practice, even with the one rather obscure mention of them in Mark 16:18. So many cultures symbolize snakes as shrewd, mysterious, and evil. It's not only Genesis 3 that speaks to this, but there's the serpent-ancestor of the Aztecs. In parts of Hinduism, there is the serpent Ananta, and we won't even try to mention the various beliefs about snakes within many African religions. But Jesus doesn't quote another religion's story on a serpent, nor does he reference Genesis 3 from his tradition. He digs much deeper into the Torah.

We find faint hints and echoes of God's ultimate purpose throughout the Old Testament. Many examples are from the prophets who foretold of a coming Messiah, and we hear many of those lessons during the Advent season. Most folks have the latter part of Isaiah memorized simply from hearing the same readings at church or listening to Handel's *Messiah* each December. But when Jesus is looking for an example to tell Nicodemus, the Torah scholar, what God is doing through him, he quotes Numbers 21:5–8.

The short and sweet of it is the Israelites complained about their conditions in the wilderness, which irked God to the point of sending poisonous snakes into the camp to teach them a lesson. The people begged Moses to make it stop, so God commanded him to create a bronze serpent on a pole, and when someone was bitten, they could look at the bronze serpent and live.

This may seem like an odd passage to quote, and Nicodemus was likely scratching his head a bit too. But when Jesus thought about what he would do on the cross, this was the image that came to mind. Of all the prophecies about the Messiah, Jesus mentions none of them; instead, he likens himself to a bronze snake on a pole.

The world is infected with a terminal disease none of us can escape. We have all been bitten by this serpent of sin, but Jesus points our eyes upward. If we look to the One who was lifted up and simply believe, then we will have life—deep and lasting life.

One great theme in John's Gospel is the connection between Jesus' humiliation and glorification. For John, it is on the cross when Jesus is ridiculed, abandoned, and suffering that he is enthroned as King of the world. Everyone else may see a man dying, but John claims this is Jesus' moment of victory. We find our salvation in his suffering and death.

Jesus reminded Nicodemus in the story from Numbers it wasn't the bronze snake that saved the people. It was merely a symbol of God's healing power. God was again going to heal his people from a grave disease, but this time, it wasn't just for the grumbling Israelites but for all people, for all time. It is as if he tells Nicodemus, "When I am at my lowest, look up because that is when I will be lifted high."

Reflection: If Jesus' humiliation is his ultimate glorification, what hope does that give us when we are at our lowest moment? Does a particular time in your life come to mind?

Day 21 • JOHN 3:16-17

What is there to say about a verse covered from every angle by practically every preacher, professor, and theologian known to man?

You can find John 3:16 plastered on billboards along the highway, written on posters at football games, and referenced at every tent revival. Believers and atheists alike know its words. Though I offer nothing new about this verse, it seems an appropriate landing point in our journey with Nicodemus.

He came in the dead of night as a seeker and possibly bit off more than he could chew. Within a few moments, Jesus talked well over his head about being born again by water and the Spirit. The word that keeps coming to his mind is, "How?" In line with Zechariah, Mary, and Thomas, he, too, asks, "How can God do this?" And Jesus' answer is "Love." Love binds the three persons of the Trinity together, drove them to create the universe, and drove Jesus to be lifted high on the cross for our sake…for Nicodemus' sake.

One cannot fathom being baptized into this new birth without first considering they are being born *into* and *out of* the eternal love of the Father, Son, and Holy Spirit. Those baptismal waters not only restore the soul but are utterly transformational, charged with the presence of God's Holy Spirit. God does not come with a band-aid treatment but with new, abundant life brought forth from his sacrificial death.

Baptism is a sacrament of belonging. It tells us we belong with and to God, and God has gone to the very edge of life and death so that we might be with him.

This was how I was introduced to the idea of baptism. Growing up in the Episcopal Church, I was the odd duck who wasn't baptized as an infant. My mother was a Methodist who married an Episcopalian. She had been baptized as a teenager in the small creek next to her church. She wanted me to remember my baptism, too. Around five-years-old, I began asking about communion and why I only received a blessing when the priest went by with the bread. The Eucharist was then an entryway for my parents to talk about the gift of baptism.

Along with them, my childhood priest told me God loved me and wanted me to be a part of his family. Communion was a family meal that reminded us of God's love each time we gathered. I told them I wanted to be a part of this family so I could share in the family meal.

A few months later, when I stood at the top of a small stepladder and leaned my head over for Father Gene Wise to baptize me, a friend my age looked at me and said, "Aren't you a little old for this?"

Years later, after I had baptized a baby during a Sunday service, a ten-year-old boy looked at his grandmother and told her he wanted to be baptized but wasn't sure if I could pick him up. She chuckled and told him that being picked up by the priest was not a requirement.

There are no roadblocks to baptism because there are no roadblocks to God. No height requirements or ID checks as we make our way to the font. Just a willing soul ready to be made new by the power of God is needed. We can have him if we want him because, ultimately, we belong.

Our friend Nicodemus seemingly disappears from the Gospel narrative, fading into the darkness of that night. Years go by, but then he mysteriously reappears at the foot of the cross. John tells us he shows up with myrrh and aloes, as was the custom for burials, and helps Joseph of Arimathea take Jesus' body off the cross and lays him in the tomb.

When all the disciples had fearfully run away into the darkness of disbelief, Nicodemus walked into the light. He had been transformed from a seeker who hid in the shadows and reappeared as a disciple of the Crucified One. I believe he could walk into the light because he had been walking in that direction all along. Jesus' words stuck with him; God really loved him to the very end of life.

Reflection: How have you experienced God's love and faithfulness? In what ways are you like Nicodemus?

week 4
LIVING WATER

Day 22 • JOHN 4:5-6

On the eastern edge of the small West Bank town of Nablus, there is a beautiful Greek Orthodox Church that rises over the local shops that surround it. Churches have come and gone on this site since the fourth century when Helena, Constantine's mother, built the first structure. In the tumultuous history of that city, the church was usually one spoil of victory for invading conquerors who delighted in tearing it down. Even a revolt led by citizens of Nablus demolished the church in the fifteenth century.[30]

Entering the solitude of the nave, adorned with icons on every wall, visitors today would never guess that so much destruction had taken place on such holy ground. Believers of the three major religions stream through their doors every year because of what lies below ground in the church's crypt. Just in front of the altar is a stairway that leads down to the church's prized jewel, a well they claim the great patriarch Jacob used. You see, Nablus used to be known as Sychar, the very heart of ancient Samaria, and it is where we find Jesus in our lesson from John 4.

The division between Jews and Samaritans has been well documented, with the former considering the latter to be half-breeds. The Samaritans were some of the poorest of the poor who were left behind during the exile to Babylon. All alone in the land, many intermarried with Gentiles. Because the Jerusalem Temple had been destroyed, they worshiped on Mount Gerizim. When the Jewish exiles returned from Babylon, the Samaritans did not welcome their arrival. The Jewish exiles returned the favor by claiming the Samaritans were not true Jews.

Geographically, Samaria was sandwiched between Galilee to the north and Jerusalem to the south. Jews in Galilee had to choose when they headed south to the Holy City for a seasonal festival. Do you take the long route along the Jordan River or risk cutting through Samaria? Most didn't want to take a chance of getting beat up and robbed (like the man in Jesus' Good Samaritan parable). And so, we should be scratching our heads and asking why Jesus would put himself and his disciples in such danger. They are unwelcomed visitors in enemy territory.

---

[30] Heba Hrimat, "The Church of Jacob's Well," *Jerusalem Patriarchate*, April 16, 2017, https://en.jerusalem-patriarchate.info/blog/2017/06/04/the-church-of-jacobs-well

But in this trip, Jesus appears not to use Samaria as a shortcut to Jerusalem, rather it is his destination. He has come there for a particular reason, risks and all. This seems to be right in line with Jesus' character. If he associated with unwelcomed people, we shouldn't be surprised he's willing to venture into uncomfortable places as well. We can no longer simply pay attention to Jesus' words. We must carefully see where he goes. He is willing to stretch himself, but more importantly, he'll stretch his disciples as he expands the message of God's kingdom outside the boundaries of Israel proper.

Ruth's words come to mind: "Where you go I will go, and where you stay I will stay" (Ruth 1:16 NIV). Leaning into uncomfortable situations where we are the minority or simply not welcomed would typically make us run in the opposite direction. But following Jesus may suggest we cannot skirt around the Samaria of our lives. The path along the Jordan is not always open, and we must venture into the land of the "other."

Reflection: Who are the "others" in your life? How might God challenge you to enter the Samaria within your community?

Day 23 • JOHN 4:7-10

Samaria: strike one. Talking to a woman: strike two. Doing it alone: strike three, and you might as well be thrown out of the game. What was Jesus thinking? He's not simply bending the rules; he is breaking every cultural norm. A good Jew would never put himself in such a precarious position. Has he not been trained in safeguarding God's People? This could ruin his reputation.

But we could say the same for the woman. In the preceding verse, we are told it is the sixth hour, meaning high noon. All the other women of the town had already come to the well in the cool of the morning, and they would return in the evening. One only goes to the well in the heat of the day to avoid bumping into anyone else. Jesus will uncover her past soon enough, but her timing already conveys her reputation. She isn't going with friends to fill up her jar, and thus she is not participating in one of the village's important daily social routines.

Wells continue to play an important role in many communities. While visiting central Tanzania, a friend took me on a tour of his large farm. He had multiple wells on his property and brought me to one he'd been digging for years. It was not only expensive but could be dangerous without the right equipment. The region had been experiencing a severe drought, so there was no guarantee this particular well would offer much water. Other wells in the area were unsafe to drink because of the pesticides used in farming. But one doesn't have to travel to east Africa to experience this. The western United States has had the same problems amid severe droughts. But as we can tell from the Gospel passage, wells were not only a necessity, but they also offered a social opportunity.

Jesus' conversation with this Samaritan woman is both functional and social. "I need water," he says to quench his thirst, but that request leads to a much deeper conversation. Again, we see a glimpse of Jesus' humanity in this passage. He comes to the woman in need. Because he was traveling, he wouldn't have brought a clay jar with him, and his disciples likely took the leather flask with them when they went into town. Though some translations make Jesus sound commanding in his request, others point out the Greek grammar urges us to put a question mark and a "please" in English. "Would you please give me a drink of water?"[31]

---

[31] Frederick Dale Bruner, *The Gospel of John: A Commentary* (Eerdmans, 2012), 245.

This simple question opens an opportunity for dialogue amid stark differences. But just like Nicodemus, this woman cannot help but ask, "How?" "How can you, a Jewish man, ask water from me, a Samaritan woman?" (See John 4:9). This sets the scene for Jesus' teaching on living water, but we would be remiss if we didn't recognize what Jesus was up to with this simple request for water. He has come as one in need, seeking help from an outcast. The woman came so that no one would see her—so that she didn't feel the shame of everyone watching her and saying nothing. But Jesus sees her, truly sees her and asks for her help.

We are not prisoners of our shame, at least we don't have to be. For everyone who has ever felt they are invisible to the world, isolated, and alone, Jesus calls out to them in the heat of the day. He sees us, and though we may not realize it at first, what he gives us far surpasses anything we might offer him. From his well, we shall draw up living water.

Reflection: How has Jesus met you in a moment of pain or isolation in your life?

Day 24 • JOHN 4:11-15

Without water, there is no life. H2O makes up 60 percent of the human body, and it composes a whopping 73 percent of our heart and brain.[32] Jesus first asks the woman for this kind of water, but he quickly turns to his main point: the living water that endures. The term "living water" was familiar to the woman. It's what we today call running water. It was considered safer than what would be in a cistern or an idle pond. Did Jesus know of a well or creek that wouldn't dry up during a drought? This could be breaking news for the village.

But Jesus has quickly moved the conversation to the deep end of the theological pool. Ancient civilizations recognized both the necessity of water and its inherent danger. All the great empires were situated along a great river, like the Tigris, Euphrates, or Nile.

But water also represented chaos and destruction. The themes of the primordial water can be found in Mesopotamian mythology as well as the first page of the Bible. The Spirit of God hovered over the watery chaos at creation (Genesis 1:2). He created its boundaries on Earth and in the sky (Genesis 1:6), and do we even need to mention Noah and the Flood? The story of Noah, at the very least, shows another ancient belief about water; it was not only a force for destruction, but it could purify and cleanse as well. God uses water to wash the world clean of the deep sin humans have created.

When Jesus tells the woman about the living water he offers, he touches on all three facets: water is life-giving, destructive, and purifying. These are also the three aspects of baptism, though in a different order. As we have already mentioned, in baptism, we die with Christ, we are washed and purified in God's redeeming action, and thus we rise with him as a new creation.

Just as Genesis 1 showed God is Lord of even the water, Jesus displays his Lordship when he offers this new, living water to the Samaritan woman. The water he speaks of is not himself. He says he is the Bread of Life, the True Vine, the Good Shepherd, but nowhere does he say he is the living water. Bruner makes this point in his *John* Commentary.[33] Rather, it is the Holy Spirit who is this life-giving water that wells up from within. The same Spirit who hovered

---

[32] Water Science School, "The Water in You: Water and the Human Body," USGS, May 22, 2019, https://www.usgs.gov/special-topics/water-science-school/science/water-you-water-and-human-body
[33] Frederick Dale Bruner, *The Gospel of John: A Commentary* (Eerdmans, 2012).

over the "wild and waste" (tohu va-vohu in Hebrew)[34] at the beginning is now willing to not only hover but to go as far as dwell in the hearts of believers. The Spirit who brings order out of chaos, life out of death, is freely offered to those who come to God's well of deep, lasting life. If our physical bodies need water to live, how much more so do believers need living water, the very Spirit of God?

On this Christian journey, we may be parched along the way, but we don't have to stay like that for long. When we drink the water he offers, we slowly become more like the man leaning on Jacob's well. It is the Son who hands us the jar; it is the Spirit that we drink, and we are transformed from the inside out.

Reflection: What do you thirst for? How might God be trying to reshape what you desire?

Day 25 • JOHN 4:16-26

Where do you go to pray? Many of us have a certain room in the house or walking path that has inevitably turned into our prayer spot. It may even be the pew we've sat in for years at church. That place matters, especially in our prayer life. We build beautiful churches because we believe there is something about sacred space; walking into that kind of place helps us shift our mindset toward something bigger than ourselves as worship. These holy spaces don't have to be massive to communicate this great truth; they simply have to be set apart—made holy—for the important work of prayer and worship.

Psychologists and theologians alike have recognized the power of place, but few have been more profound on this topic than the Kentucky farmer and author, Wendell Berry. He has been a prophetic voice to a generation that is seemingly in a perpetual hurry. Spending a lifetime tending the same fields and walking in the same woods has deeply shaped how he sees the world and our place in it. One of his Sabbath poems ends like this:

> "His land—this meager sod,
> These stones, this low estate—
> Is the household of God.
> And it is Heaven's gate."[35]

Place matters deeply to us. Whether we are conscious of it or not, we are shaped by our surroundings, from the places we fall on our knees in prayer to the meager sod we trample on daily.

I remember intently watching the live news coverage of Notre Dame Cathedral burning. It was like witnessing someone die a slow death. It was sickening to see such a beautiful church consumed in flames after having stood the test of time for so long. We are reminded of the fragility of our sacred spaces. We move homes and must find a new prayer corner. We move churches and must find a new pew. In those times of change, we are reminded that place is given its significance by the One who created all places. Churches and nature point us to Something or Someone bigger, deeper, and eternal.

This is essentially Jesus' response to the woman. In telling her that he knows her past and her current living arrangements, she then redirects the conversation to the age-old debate between Samaritans and Jews. Does God

---

[35] Wendell Berry, *This Day: Collected & New Sabbath Poems* (Counterpoint, 2014), 250.

intend to be worshiped in Jerusalem or Mount Gerizim? Jesus goes along with the question, but he tells the woman that soon enough, it will not matter on which mountain they worship because "true worshipers will worship the Father in spirit and truth" (John 4:23). Jesus wasn't telling her those two holy places didn't matter, but he was expanding her vision of the sacred to the very sod and stones on which she was currently standing. God is not limited to Gerizim or Zion; as Spirit, all people from all places would worship him.

Jesus then takes it one step further. He tells her he is the long-awaited "Ta'eb," the word Samaritans used for the Messiah. But, on top of that, he says, "I who speak to you am he" (v. 26). Just as God told Moses his name was, "I AM WHO I AM," on Mount Sinai, Jesus reveals to this unnamed Samaritan that she is in the presence of the great I AM. She need not go to the top of Mount Gerizim to find the God of Abraham, Isaac, and Jacob; no, he is standing right in front of her.

The Holy of Holies has come to her and met her in her pain, isolation, and shame. God has never been held captive in a temple or church—he is always on the loose and meeting people where they are. We should never be surprised when God meets us in the ordinary places of our lives, among the humdrum routines that make up so much of our days. Places and sacred space matter, but we should never forget God meets us where we are and calls us to look for him in some of the most common places of our lives.

Reflection: What places are special to you and why? Has God met you in some surprising places?

Day 26 · JOHN 4:27-30

In my first couple of years out of seminary, there was one important aspect of ministry I struggled with mightily. I had a hard time inviting people. I'm not even talking about inviting people outside the church to come to visit my church; I struggled, even inviting parishioners into ministry opportunities within our church. I kept telling myself people were too busy or they lived too far away to join a new initiative I wanted to start. I feared being rejected, and in those early years, our church was severely limited because I wouldn't ask people to share in the ministries of the parish.

It took a while, and a few tough conversations with some wise mentors, to realize that what I wanted to invite people into was not a burden. Inviting people into ministry validates the person being asked and inspires others to join. Healthy ministries (and ministers) have a multiplication effect. People want to make a difference and be a part of something special. In this case, I was the roadblock to God's action in that church. When we started inviting more folks to participate in the life of the church, it quickly flourished. The handful of "no's" we received didn't come close to the numerous people who joyfully said yes.

It really is astounding how quickly the Samaritan woman has changed her tune in our Gospel passage. This short conversation with Jesus has turned into a full-on conversion. She went to the well looking for water, and she found something much better. She left her water jar at the well and quickly ran back to the town to share with her neighbors the living water she had just received.

If Jesus knew her past, there is no doubt the townspeople did, too. They had seen it play out over the years right in front of them. But this living-water-filled woman is not limited to her past. She will not let anything stop her from inviting people to come to see the man who just may be the Christ. In some ways, she has brought this new kind of well, filled with this new kind of water, directly to them. She has tasted the water herself and has been transformed into a gushing spring of deep, lasting water.

The specific invitation she makes to her neighbors is, "Come and see." There are no theological arguments. She doesn't hand out a bullet point list of what Jesus teaches; rather, it's a simple request to go with her to see this man who told her everything she had done.

This is not the first time an invitation like this has been made. In John 1, it appears two times. A couple of John the Baptist's disciples decide to follow Jesus after being told he is the Lamb of God. Along the way, they ask Jesus where he is staying, and his simple response is, "Come and see" (John 1:39). A few verses later, Philip tells Nathaniel they have found the one whom Moses and the prophets foretold, and that he is a Nazarene. Nathaniel retorts, "Can anything good come out of Nazareth?" Philip doesn't skip a beat and says, "Come and see" (John 1:43–51).

Many of us have come to faith (or remained in faith) because of someone who has invited us, like Philip or the Samaritan woman. They may not have all the answers or doctrines and dogmas down pat, but they know Christ and make him known.

In a recent conversation I had with a group of young adults, the main reason they do not share their faith with others is due to fear of not being able to answer all the questions they may be asked. If only Jesus cared that we knew all the answers. What he wants more than anything else is that we know him.

At the heart of baptismal living is an invitation to come and see. See for yourself if this man is who he claims to be. Come and see he is good and worthy of our trust. Like the woman, we may come to the well looking for water, and go home with an overflowing spring of new and abundant life.

Reflection: Who invited you to come and see the goodness of God? How might you be able to live into this baptismal call to invite others as well?

Day 27 • JOHN 4:31-38

If our passage was a movie scene, there would be a "crosscut" to show what Jesus and the disciples were up to while the woman has gone to town. The crowded village would slowly fade from view, and the camera would zoom in on the scene back at the well. There is a similarity in this conversation to the one Jesus had with the woman earlier, but instead of discussing water, the topic is now about food.

The disciples are worried their rabbi hasn't eaten. While they are concerned about physical food, Jesus, yet again, is thinking spiritually deeper. Who needs food when you're doing the Father's work? The field is ripe for harvest, and there are some who are already reaping what has been sown.

As Dale Bruner says, the Jewish proverb Jesus quotes, "There are yet four months, then comes the harvest," is equivalent to us saying, "Rome wasn't built in a day."[36] It takes a lot of time for something to grow to maturity. The whole summer is spent waiting for harvest time. Hours upon hours are spent just for that moment when you can taste the fruit of all that labor. My grandparents used to have a decorative sign in one of their potted plants that said, "Grow Dang It!" You just can't wish for something to grow; time is a key ingredient.

But Jesus says there are times of instant results when the sower and reaper can rejoice together. Miracles happen, and the disciples unknowingly find themselves in one. The field is ripe for harvest, and who would've thought Samaria would be one of the first places to be reaped?

Working in the fields for the sake of the Gospel can be challenging. It is labor-intensive and time-consuming because we are dealing with people. The field we are called to tend faithfully is the relationships we have (or should have). But we must remember who called us into the harvest field in the first place.

We would be remiss not to connect this passage with Jesus' saying in the Gospel of Matthew, "And Jesus went throughout all the cities and villages, teaching in their synagogues and proclaiming the gospel of the kingdom and healing every disease and every affliction. When he saw the crowds, he had compassion for them, because they were harassed and helpless, like sheep without a shepherd.

---

[36] Dale Bruner, *The Gospel of John: A Commentary* (Eerdmans, 2012), 275.

Then he said to his disciples, 'The harvest is plentiful, but the laborers are few; therefore pray earnestly to the Lord of the harvest to send out laborers into his harvest'" (9:35–38).

Back at the well, Jesus is looking at his loyal followers and saying, "I just sent out one laborer, and look in the distance; you can see the whole town is heading this way! The harvest is at hand, and it's yours to reap with me if you are willing to get to work."

Jesus reminds us people may be more receptive to the Gospel than we think. Much of the work we do in Jesus' name may be a slow go of it, and we may never see any visible fruit come to bear. At the same time, we shouldn't be surprised when people quickly receive the good news with joy. It simply means God has been working on them for a long time, and this is the moment it has all come together. We must trust that Jesus truly is the Lord of the harvest. The relationships and conversations we cultivate over a lifetime are worth it because we know the true Sower of the field, and he will bring all things to bear in his good time.

Reflection: Are you a patient person? How have you seen God work in slow ways? Have you seen God work quickly as well?

Day 28 • JOHN 4:39-42

My college New Testament professor, Dr. Roger Green, defined faith this way: "Faith is taking everything you know about yourself and committing it to everything you know about God." This one sentence has carried me through some tough days in my life. Faith is hard, and it does not always come naturally.

I shared this quote with a friend struggling with his faith over the past few months. He's been asking a lot of questions, which has led to some doubts. In the long run, these questions will only strengthen his faith, but in the present moment, it has left him a little unsettled. In our conversation, he began to worry about the certainty of the Christian claims, and I had to remind him that faith offers a different kind of assurance.

Like the woman at the well, my friend was looking for something tangible and what Jesus offers is eternal. I wish I had told him that what Jesus offers is living water, but instead, Dr. Green's quote came to mind. Committing everything you know about yourself into the hands of a good and gracious God first means you must do some serious soul-searching. If you don't really know yourself, there's not much to entrust to God.

The Samaritan woman is yet again a great example for us. She knew herself and her past, and she recognized Jesus knew all of it as well, and he still offered this new, living water to her. Because of the grace she received, she has turned into a walking fountain of living water. The Samaritan townspeople have taken one sip and want to meet the Source.

Simply based on this woman's testimony, the town has come to faith in this unseen man at the well. This is so shocking, in part, because Jesus is usually greeted with skepticism and contempt. Usually, he is asked where he came from or where he got his authority. When the Samaritans finally meet him, they ask no prying questions. Rather, the first thing out of their mouths is an invitation to stay with them. A Jew traveling through this region was risky; a Jew being welcomed as an honored guest in Samaria was unheard of. This living water Jesus offered had broken down a cultural and religious dam, and the good news that God's kingdom had finally arrived flooded the whole town.

When the town invites Jesus to stay with them, the old English word that is sometimes used is "abide." Later, Jesus will tell his disciples to abide in him because he is the True Vine (John 15:4). But at this moment, the Samaritans are aware enough not to let Jesus simply walk away. If given the chance, they will welcome him into their home. By showing hospitality in this way to a stranger, we could call them the Good Samaritans. Jesus has received more acceptance outside of Israel than within—a great reminder that even though Jesus' central focus in his ministry was his fellow Jews, his message will transcend borders and cultures.

But we must not forget the town's faith came through the testimony of a woman with a troubled past. Her past would not define her. Instead, we remember her for her faith. She took what little she knew about this rabbi and everything she knew about herself and jumped headfirst into the living water of God's grace. She will forever be known as Samaria's first evangelist and one of the very first missionaries commissioned by Jesus himself.

Though she fades from the biblical story after this passage, it is hard not to imagine the great impact she had on her town once Jesus left. What began as an awkward encounter at the edge of town turned into a life-changing experience. A little faith can make all the difference.

Reflection: What do you need to entrust to Jesus today?

week 5
NEW EYES

Day 29 • JOHN 9:1-5

Every sport has its unique quirks. Football has hours of pregame tailgating, soccer has its chants that ring throughout the stadium, and baseball has its superstitions. A lot of athletes have certain things they do on game day, but baseball players take it to another level.

I frequently watch baseball games. Over the years, I have seen some patterns: shortstop Nomar Garciaparra went through a meticulous process of adjusting his batting gloves before each pitch, pitcher Tim Wakefield would eat a pound of spaghetti before every game he started, and the 2019 Washington Nationals wore the same blue jersey through the playoffs because they kept winning when wearing it—they ended up World Series champions. As a pitcher in college, I had my own strange routines, like jumping over the chalk baseline before heading back to the dugout.

I sometimes found it hard to reconcile my game day superstitions with my Christian beliefs. I knew victory wasn't determined by if I put my left sock on before the other, but it had become a ritual of sorts, ensuring I'd play well. It's also amazing how many of us believe in karma in one form or fashion. Though many Christians have never read any official Hindu or Buddhist beliefs on the matter, so many of us unconsciously ascribe to the broad teachings of cause and effect found in the teachings of karma. It gives us a rational answer to suffering by saying there are consequences to our actions. Why do bad things happen to good people? Because they did something to deserve it. We believe in fairness and justice, don't we?

The disciples are wrestling with this question as they walk past a blind man. They ask Jesus about his ailment—within earshot of the man, no less. They assume his (or his family's) sin is the root cause of his blindness. While the disciples see a theological problem, Jesus sees a person. The Bible does not give the full answer of why good people suffer and why bad people do not always get caught. Jesus uses this opportunity to raise up a man cast down by society and to display his true sight amid such blatant spiritual blindness.

This may be one of the most well-crafted stories in any of the Gospels, and its theme is quite simple: who sinned and who sees? Some commentators, like Bruner, believe the man represents humanity apart from Christ. Jesus gives true sight to all those who are blinded by sin. The disciples were better off sitting next to the blind man, and then asking Jesus why they were all blind—physically or spiritually—instead of assuming they were better off than he was. From this point on, it will be the blind man who teaches the disciples and the religious leaders about faith and sight.

In these five verses, we do not learn why bad things happen to good people, but we are reminded God sees us, truly sees us, even in our darkest moments. Though we may turn a blind eye to some of those around us, our Lord is not blind to the plight of the needy. Our God is one who does not turn away. He doesn't see a problem; instead, he sees a person. And in the end, Jesus allowed a lot of bad things to happen to him, though he didn't deserve it. His pain validates our pain. Not even God would skirt around suffering and death. He addresses it head on, so that his light would break through sin and darkness once and for all.

Reflection: How have you reckoned with why bad things happen to good people in your mind? What's the most challenging aspect of it? What have you been taught is the Christian response to that problem?

Day 30 • JOHN 9:6-7

A few years ago, I had a conversation with a preacher who used to serve a church in Baltimore. They had a policy that acolytes (the children who participated in the service) had to wear black shoes. All the acolytes wore the same vestments during the service, and the church was adamant the children shouldn't walk down the aisle in flip-flops or dirty sneakers. Uniformity was the name of the game. The church had a few extra pairs of black shoes, just in case someone forgot to bring their own.

One day, a middle school girl invited her friend to come to this church with her. Her friend confessed she'd like to go but didn't know if she had nice enough clothes to attend. Thinking about the white robes and black shoes in the vesting room, the young lady piped up, "Oh, the church will dress you up just fine." She was right in more ways than one.

Christians have always claimed something happens in baptism. Paul says in some mysterious way we die with Christ in baptism and rise to new life in him. He says in Romans, "We were buried therefore with him by baptism into death, in order that, just as Christ was raised from the dead by the glory of the Father, we too might walk in newness of life" (6:4).

Ephrem, the Syrian, claimed Jesus deposited his eternal robe of glory in the baptismal waters so that in our baptism we would be clothed in his robe of glory.[37] It is much more than a ritual washing; God's Holy Spirit changes and transforms us in baptism. It is God's action within baptism that makes all the difference. It is God who clothes us with his righteousness and grace.

You can then see how the early Church fathers came to believe the pool of Siloam in John 9 prefigured Christian baptism. As God breathed life into the dust and created Adam, so now Jesus uses dust and saliva to anoint the blind man's eyes. Jesus then sends him to wash in a pool connected to a messianic prophecy. It was said Jews drew water from this pool during the Feast of Tabernacles to symbolize the blessings expected when the Messiah finally arrived.[38] And so, the man out of faithful obedience to Jesus (the One sent from God) goes to the pool called "Sent," while there he is made new in the act of washing, and then he is sent to tell what Jesus has done.

---

[37] Sebastian Brock, "The Robe of Glory – A Biblical Image in the Syriac Tradition," *The Way*, https://www.theway.org.uk/back/39Brock.pdf Accessed December 9, 2022.
[38] Henry Wansbrough, ed., *The New Jerusalem Bible* (New York: Doubleday, 1985) Note e

This story has a missionary spirit. A person is called into baptism by the overwhelming action of God (what we like to call grace); clothed, restored, and made whole in baptism, and then he is sent out as an agent of God's kingdom. The baptized are always empowered to go out and be witnesses of God's action in the world.

At the heart of this missionary spirit is obedience. At any point, the man could have brushed Jesus off, but for some reason he went, he washed, and then he saw. This washing allowed him to see Jesus, and everything else, with a new sense of clarity. Each of our personal baptism stories may be different, but the three steps are constant for all. We went, we washed, and now we see things with a new perspective. As Chrysostom once said, "As then Christ was the spiritual rock, so also was he the spiritual Siloam."[39]

The young lady in Baltimore was right: the church will dress you just fine by offering Jesus' robe of glory for each of us to put on. But through the spiritual Siloam, we are given not only a new wardrobe but also a new lens to look through—one that will help us see the Lord's great work happening right in front of us.

Reflection: How has the Lord opened your eyes in years past? What did that experience teach you?

---

[39] Chrysostom, "Homily 57 on the Gospel of John," *New Advent*, https://www.newadvent.org/fathers/240157.htm Accessed December 13, 2022.

Day 31 • JOHN 9:8-12

What do you think people say behind your back? Some of us are more paranoid than others, but occasionally I think many wonder what people really think of us. Labeling people in grade school was pretty easy. It usually depended on who you sat next to in the cafeteria. There's the football team in one corner, the artists and theater kids in another, and nerds and gamers huddled around one another. It was easy to label people at that age because we all desperately wanted to fit into a group.

Adulthood is a little more subtle. Our glory days on the athletic field are behind us, so hopefully we're not still wearing our letterman jackets. And hopefully we are not trying to belong through fashion or hairstyles either. Yet, we still have labels we put on people: conservative or liberal, successful or failure, rich or poor. We hold on to labels people have given us, or we have imposed on ourselves. They can define our self-worth and shape the kind of people we become.

For the man with his new sight, a lot had changed in a short time. He went from never having seen anything to instantly soaking everything in. He was seeing his hometown for the first time, and as he walked down the street, he matched his neighbors' voices with their faces (probably shocked at how they really looked).

He was used to hearing people talk about him, but now he could see the confusion on their faces as he looked right at them and smiled. "Is that the blind man? Is that the beggar sitting along the road this morning?"

The man claims it and says, "I am that man." He has agency in a way he didn't before. He can look his neighbors in the eye and claim with confidence that he is the one they speak about. There's no need for them to whisper behind his back anymore.

But why were his neighbors so confused? His eyes were opened, but it didn't say he received a full makeover. How could they not recognize him? I doubt it was his physical appearance that baffled them, rather it was the shock of the moment and what this healing signified if it were true. Blind people don't receive their sight, even those who wash in the pool of Siloam. This was a first. As the townspeople tried to process the news of this miracle, they likely thought of God's promise in Isaiah to "open eyes that are blind, to free captives from prison and to release from the dungeon those who sit in darkness" (42:7 NIV).

It was God who opened the eyes of the blind, and now this beggar says a stranger healed him. How can this be?

For the average first-century Jew who knew the Law and the Prophets, this miracle would've raised some alarm bells. Something was afoot, and God had to be involved for something this amazing to occur. At the center of the town's mystery is this newly healed "seeing man." Now the main topic of everyone's conversation, it doesn't seem to faze him. He doesn't exaggerate the story, nor does he put himself at the center of it. Even at the most transformational moment of his life, where he is finally the talk of the town, he simply tells his neighbors what Jesus has done for him. This is a valuable lesson for each of us on faith, honesty, and a whole lot of humility. May we follow his glorious example.

Reflection: It matters more what God says about us than what others do. How have you dealt with labels that others (or you yourself) have put on you?

Day 32 • JOHN 9:13-17

There is a pivotal moment in many people's life when they finally admit to themselves they need contacts or glasses. It's always a hard reality to accept. For me, I realized my eyesight was bad when I couldn't see the players' numbers at a Vanderbilt University basketball game. It didn't help that I was sitting way up in the third deck. I then realized I had a lot of places in my life where I was struggling to see (and maybe that was the reason I was striking out so much in baseball). Soon enough, I went to see a family friend who was an optometrist in town, and within an hour, I could see clearly again. It was a miracle.

We seek the counsel of experts all the time. We go see doctors who know about the human body, CPAs who know taxes, and mechanics who know their way around a car. The Pharisees were the religious experts of the day. If you had any questions concerning faith, you'd seek their counsel. A blind man walking around town saying some person named Jesus healed him would've been a good reason to get the religious experts involved. The citizens of that town knew what the Prophet Isaiah foretold about the blind receiving their sight, but the Pharisees would've *really* known the prophecy inside and out. Of course, they could bring some clarity to the situation.

But just as quickly as they begin their investigation, some have already concluded: "This man is not from God, for he does not keep the Sabbath" (John 9:16). It's a clear-cut case for them. This man is a Sabbath-breaker, and God would never work through someone like that.

A few others in the crowd couldn't accept a sinner could do such a miracle as this. Surely, he was a man of God. Though the two factions may disagree on how this mystery man has such power, they are both deeply concerned. They were the experts, and someone has been doing deeds of God right under their noses. He didn't even ask for their permission!

This was a perceived threat from within their ranks, which likely raised their anxieties. They knew how to put down the silly pagan beliefs of the Romans, and they could easily brush aside more extreme branches of their faith, like those in Qumran, but this was different. Here was a Jew who seemed to be inaugurating Isaiah's vision, and possibly the beginning of the Messiah's reign. How could this be? They were the experts of God's Word, and certainly they would be the first to detect something this monumental was beginning.

How could they be so blind?

John wants us to see the irony of this story. The kingdom of God is turning the world upside down. The last are becoming first, and the blind see clearly while the experts are left wandering in the dark.

With each new question, the seeing man's vision of Jesus expands into a fuller picture. At first, he told his neighbors a *man* healed him, and now he tells the Pharisees it was a *prophet* who did this great wonder. Like the Samaritan woman, his vision becomes clearer, more attuned to what God is up to. She too said, "Sir, I perceive that you are a prophet" (John 4:19).

Let's be clear. The Pharisees are not inherently bad. Like all of us, they want to have clear boundaries and know what is permissible and what is not. Life—and especially faith—are not a free-for-all. And as we know, introducing something new can be threatening to the status quo. If you uphold the existing state of affairs, then you'll do everything in your power to keep it that way.

As unsettling as it was for them, Jesus was shaking the very foundations on which their confidence rested. Things would change, but in reality, things were always going to change when the Messiah arrived. Jesus wasn't turning the world upside down as much as he was turning it right-side up as N.T. Wright often says. The Pharisees just happened to be caught up in this radical reordering, and the blind were showing them how to see clearly for the first time.

Reflection: Has there been a time your eyes were opened to God's work by an unlikely person? What was that experience like, and what did you learn?

Day 33 • JOHN 9:18-23

Fear is a powerful motivator. Talk to any therapist, and they will tell you how fear shapes many of our thoughts and actions. It is what kept our cave-dwelling ancestors alive, and it keeps us awake in the early morning hours as we're finishing a project due that day. When properly used, it can be quite helpful, but more times than not, fear stops us in our tracks.

In a great scene in *The Wizard of Oz*, the Cowardly Lion says, "All right, I'll go in there for Dorothy. Wicked Witch or no Wicked Witch, guards or no guards, I'll tear them apart. I may not come out alive, but I'm going in there. There's only one thing I want you fellows to do."

"What's that?" the Tin Man and Scarecrow ask.
The Cowardly Lion replies, "Talk me out of it!"[40]

I'm more like the Cowardly Lion than I want to admit. We can hypothesize how we'll be under pressure, but we really don't know until we're presented with a particular challenge. Thus far, the seeing man in our passage has been fearlessly truthful—a quality that becomes even more endearing as the story goes on. It is the Pharisees who seem worried, but they pour all their angst onto the poor man's parents.

A sympathetic reading of the parents' actions would say that so much had changed in a short time. They were still trying to wrap their head around this miracle. Yes, that was their son, but how could this be? They did not wake up that morning expecting their son to be healed by a traveling rabbi.

But we could also make that case for the seeing man. His life had utterly changed in a matter of a few minutes, but he still told the truth to anyone who asked.

Fear gripped the inner circle of the Pharisees because they wondered what this all meant for them and their faith. The parents were gripped by the fear of what the Pharisees could do to them. Being cast out of the local synagogue would have essentially meant they were cast out of the village. Their home, including their friends and livelihood, was on the line. They won't win a Parents of the Year Award anytime soon for their answer, essentially punting the question back to their son, but this wouldn't be the last time Jesus would put his followers in a costly situation.

[40] Simran Khurana, "Quotes about Courage from the Cowardly Lion," *Live About*, January 14, 2020. https://www.liveabout.com/find-the-lion-within-you-2832238

For all of us, there comes a moment when we must decide who Jesus really is, come what may. Many over the centuries have lost their lives for their profession of faith. For others, it may cost a relationship, a job opportunity, or social standing. But for each of us, it comes down to being dictated by fear or faith.

It's hard not to think about Dietrich Bonhoeffer's stance against the Nazis, which ended with his execution, or Archbishop Desmond Tutu fearlessly standing against the apartheid government in South Africa and being a voice of hope and forgiveness when the new government was established.

Archbishop Oscar Romero became a voice for the oppressed in El Salvador, and in one sermon preached directly to the military. He said, "I want to make a special appeal to soldiers, national guardsmen, and policemen: each of you is one of us. The peasants you kill are your own brothers and sisters. When you hear a man telling you to kill, remember God's words, 'thou shalt not kill.'...In the name of God, in the name of our tormented people, I beseech you, I implore you; in the name of God, I command you to stop the repression."[41] The next day, he was shot down while celebrating Mass.

We can criticize the seeing man's parents because of their fear, but it may be more beneficial for us to take a good look in the mirror and then drop to our knees in prayer. As the old hymn goes,
"Save us from weak resignation
to the evils we deplore;
let the gift of your salvation
be our glory evermore.
Grant us wisdom, grant us courage
serving thee whom we adore,
serving thee whom we adore."[42]

God, the giver of wisdom and courage, can fill in the gap when we are weak. We mustn't think we should magically stir up bravery within ourselves. As Moses told the Israelites, "Be strong and courageous. Do not fear or be in dread of them, for it is the LORD your God who goes with you. He will not leave you or forsake you" (Deuteronomy 31:6a).

Thankfully, courageous faith comes from the Lion of Judah and not from the Cowardly Lion.

Reflection: Do you consider yourself brave? Who are some people in your life who you would call courageous Christians? What makes them unique?

---

[41] "Archbishop Oscar Romero, *University of Notre Dame Kellogg Institute of for International Studies*, https://kellogg.nd.edu/archbishop-oscar-romero Accessed December 9, 2022.

[42] Harry Emerson Fosdick, *The Hymnal*, "God of Grace and God of Glory" (Church Publishing, 1982), Hymn 594.

Day 34 • JOHN 9:24-34

Every preacher needs another preacher in their life. What I mean is preachers need someone to speak into their lives as well. It is a great honor to climb into a pulpit week after week and proclaim the Word of God, but if I'm being honest, it can also be draining. Who am I to talk with such authority about Scripture? It is good for preachers to occasionally hear from someone else.

My personal preacher doesn't serve in a church, nor does he have a seminary degree. Jesse was one of my college baseball teammates. In many respects, we are complete opposites. I grew up in a quiet suburb surrounded by cow pastures, and he grew up near Compton in Los Angeles. He appears rough around the edges, covered in tattoos, and has a whole lot of street smarts. I, on the other hand, have zero street smarts and have been hustled a time or two. He calls me a redneck, and I call him a thug, but it's just proof you shouldn't judge a book by its cover.

When we talk, it usually gets deep quickly. Jesse has a voracious desire to learn. He reads constantly, he talks to people from many different backgrounds, and he is always reflecting on how he can grow as a person. When I'm running on empty and need to be recharged, I call Jesse. He is one of the wisest and most discerning people I know.

My parishioners may be surprised that the first person I call when I need help in ministry is not a bishop, a colleague in ministry, or a former professor—it's my old college buddy. But Jesse is a great personal preacher. He is brutally honest and prophetic in ways he doesn't even realize. Over the years, he has turned into my preacher.

It really is amazing what Jesus does when he takes root in people's lives. Education is good, and experience is great, but there's nothing like someone who is filled with the Holy Spirit. You just want to be around them all the time. We shouldn't forget the seeing man in our passage washed in a pool called "Sent." Ever since that miraculous washing, he has been a missionary for Jesus. He has gone to his neighbors and the religious authorities to tell them what Jesus has done for him. He went from begging on the streets to preaching to the preachers, all in one day.

He even gives them a theology and history lesson. He reminds them God listens to those who worship him and do his will, thus the man who healed him must not be a sinner. He then goes one step further: "Never since the world began has it been heard that anyone opened the eyes of a man born blind" (John 9:32). Surely the Pharisees know their theology and history, but as the controversy increases, this man's faith illuminates as well. He cannot help but speak honestly—even to the experts.

The Pharisees are convinced if they can find out where Jesus has come from, then they'll know his true intentions. Again, the Gospel writer John can't help but emphasize this point. Even if they knew where Jesus was truly from and who sent him, they still would not believe.

They discredit the man as being ignorant and born in utter sin. He has dared to teach the teachers, and for that, he is cast out of the synagogue. His honesty has cost him, but as St. Augustine once said, "It was no disadvantage to be put out of the synagogue: whom they cast out, Christ took in."[43]

Jesus is always waiting for us on the other side.

Reflection: Baptismal living requires good mentors who will encourage and challenge you in the faith. Godparents can play an important role in this way. What have you learned from your mentors or godparents?

---

[43] Augustine, "Tractate 44 (John 9)," *New Advent*, https://www.newadvent.org/fathers/1701044.htm Accessed December 13, 2022.

Day 35 • JOHN 9:35-41

Our passage concludes in a way I wish every Gospel story would end: with a profession of faith and a deep sense of humility. But there is a reason this story is remarkable. Out of this whole ordeal, it is one man who sees clearly while all the others are still blind.

I'm reminded of John Henry Newman's poem, "Lead Kindly Light," which embodies much of the faithfulness of the seeing man. The first stanza goes:
"Lead, Kindly Light, amid the encircling gloom,
Lead Thou me on;
The night is dark, and I am far from home,
Lead Thou me on.
Keep Thou my feet;
I do not ask to see the distant scene;
one step enough for me."[44]

The seeing man is never given a full vision of who Jesus is. He doesn't see the Mount of Transfiguration Jesus, but he doesn't have to for his faith to be authentic. He knows the power of the Almighty God healed him, and that's more than enough to warrant his trust in Jesus.

"Who is this Son of Man, so that I may believe in him?" Who says that? He is so ready to believe, so ready to give thanks for what has happened to him, that when Jesus tells him the Son of Man is speaking to him, the seeing man automatically professes him as Lord and worships him.

He is a missionary like the woman at the well, but this town did not receive him as the Samaritans received the woman. He is born again through the power of the Holy Spirit. If only Nicodemus were there to see what it looked like in the flesh. But compared to all the others, the seeing man is the first to worship Jesus as Lord. His sight is clear now, the One who stands before him is not just a man, not just a prophet; he is the Lord.

It begs the question, what is needed for faith? We live in an age of skepticism, but the Pharisees have taught us every age has had doubts about Jesus. Will miracles do the trick? Clearly not, or the whole town would have fallen down to worship of Jesus.

---

[44] John Henry Newman, "Lead Kindly Light," Public Domain

How about Scripture? If only people saw Jesus prophesied in the Bible. Not so fast. The Pharisees were the supposed experts, and not even they grasped what was happening.

What if they used their heads a little more and were a bit more rational? The blind receiving sight could only come from God, the Author and Giver of life. But why would God work through a Sabbath-breaker? It just didn't make sense. Faith doesn't offer a thorough answer to all our questions. As Rowan Williams says, "[Faith] appears quite simply in the form of 'dependable relationship.' You may not understand, or have the words on the tip of your tongue, but you learn somehow to be confident in a presence, an 'other,' who does not change or go away."[45]

Sometimes we want to see the full picture, the whole story, but God only gives us a small snapshot of his plan. We may fight it tooth and nail, demanding more evidence before we are convinced, but that is not how faith works. We must surrender to the small things, the little ways God tries to get our attention daily. The Christian journey is not a fireworks show. It is a slow walk with an abiding presence, or what Eugene Peterson called "a long obedience in the same direction" in his book with that title. One step must be enough for us because, at the very least, we know our Lord is walking right beside us.

Reflection: How have the seeing man's actions in this passage challenged or encouraged you? What will you take away from the lessons learned in John 9?

---

[45] Rowan Williams, *Being Disciples: Essentials of the Christian Life* (Eerdmans, 2016), 25.

week 6
DEATH TO LIFE

Day 36 • JOHN 1:1-4

In the weeks leading up to Easter, those who were preparing to be baptized in the ancient church (known as catechumens), would notice a shift in their teaching. For the better part of the last two or three years, they were asked to comply with the church's ethical demands. This was a moral trial of sorts as they lived out the values of the Christian community in their daily lives. They were expected to care for the sick, visit the widowed and orphaned, and deal kindly with the poor in their community.

They were to "walk the walk" for a couple of years before getting to "talk the talk." But as Easter approached, the local bishop would give them a new title and some new teachings. They would now be considered "Candidates for Baptism," and their lessons with the bishop would center on the Gospel rather than specific moral instructions.[46]

God willing, the candidates had learned over the years that the baptized were called into the mess of humanity, what one writer describes as the "neighborhood of chaos."[47] They were to learn baptism would not separate them from the world, but would actually do the opposite. It would bring them into deeper solidarity with those in turmoil. These candidates were required to learn this valuable lesson before ever cracking open the Gospels.

In the Book of Common Prayer, the Baptismal Covenant requires candidates for baptism profess what they believe by saying the Apostles' Creed, and then responding to a series of questions with: "I will with God's help."

Some of those questions go like this:
"Will you proclaim by word and example the Good News of God in Christ? Will you seek and serve Christ in all persons, loving your neighbor as yourself? Will you strive for justice and peace among all people and respect the dignity of every human being?"[48]

I've been tempted to condense all three of those questions into one by asking, "As the baptized, are you willing to enter the neighborhood of chaos and live in solidarity with your fellow human beings as Christ demands?"

---

[46] Loosely based off of Will Willimon's *Remember Who You Are: Baptism, a Model for Christian Life* (Upper Room, 1998). 17.
[47] Rowan Williams, *Being Christian: Baptism, Bible, Eucharist, Prayer* (Eerdmans, 2014), 4.
[48] *Book of Common Prayer*, (Church Publications, 1979), 305.

This may be too jarring of a question for our modern parishioners, but I doubt the ancient catechumens would've blinked an eye. They were embodying this way of living years before their baptism.

It is then so shocking in our passage that Jesus seems unconcerned with the news of Lazarus' illness. This is his good friend, whom he loves, after all. He's healed so many strangers you'd think he'd jump at the opportunity to help a friend.

It is a bit mystifying, but we can always be confident Jesus is purposeful with each of his actions—and even his inactions. There is one similarity to last week's lesson. Jesus said the man's blindness was not due to sin, but so that God's work may be displayed in him. Similarly, this illness (and momentary death) will glorify God. Poor Lazarus will have to go through all this, but like the seeing man in John 9, he will become a living testament to God's action in this world.

The baptized are called to witness to this in-breaking activity and action of God—not from the sidelines but deep in the heart of the human predicament. And no matter what, no matter how things appear, we must trust in the unmatched timing of God.

Reflection: Has there been a time when you have not trusted in God's timing or tried to rush him to act?

Day 37 • JOHN 11:5-15

In the first five years of marriage, my wife and I lived in five different places. That alone would have done some marriages in, but we seemed to adjust fairly well to each new home. We saw it as an adventure of sorts. But in our move from Nashville to Houston, we were adamant we'd put down roots for a while. My wife was three months pregnant, and so our life was about to drastically change. We needed a home to start our new family.

Unfortunately, we had trouble finding the right house. After a few months of deals falling through, we felt the clock ticking as the baby's due date drew closer. With each week, my anxiety rose, and with that, my standards also lowered. I was no longer looking for our "dream house." I would've gladly taken anything, but thankfully, my wife's patience won the day. We held out and found the right house, but only a few weeks before our baby girl arrived.

Timing is everything. Whether it's real estate or relationships, timing plays an important role. With faith, we are told to trust God's timing; he will provide when and how he wants. There is little use trying to force his hand.

Jesus' lack of urgency to attend to Lazarus gives him a chance to teach his disciples one more lesson before they head to Judea for the final time. It's only chapter 11 in John, but once he arrives in Bethany, Jesus will remain in the greater Jerusalem area until his death and resurrection. Perhaps he wanted to spend a few more days looking out at the beautiful Sea of Galilee before he turned his face to Jerusalem one last time.

His final teaching beside the sea is all about God's timing. After beating around the bush with his disciples, Jesus finally comes out with it, "Lazarus has died, and for your sake I am glad that I was not there, so that you may believe" (John 11:14–15a).

Jesus knows the days ahead will be pretty grim, especially for the disciples, who are consistently unaware of what must occur. Jesus, as a good and caring pastor, tells them he will rouse Lazarus from his deathly stupor so that they may believe.

Believe what? When the disciples see him dying on a cross and buried in a tomb, he hopes they will hold onto the image of Lazarus walking out of his tomb. Dark days lie ahead, and they will need this powerful image to get them through. Light will overcome the darkness, even when it appears death has won. This final lesson before going to Bethany is meant to plant a seed of hope.

The Greek word used in verse 12 to say Lazarus "will recover" can also be translated "will be saved."[49] Lazarus will be saved in one sense when he walks out of that tomb, and then he (and everyone else) will be saved in a deeper sense when Jesus walks out of his tomb. Jesus prays his disciples will remember this teaching as the events of Holy Week play out.

God's timing is perplexing, but it is clear he always has us in mind. James Baldwin says in his book *The Fire Next Time*, "The Lord never seems to get there when you want him, but when he arrives, he's always right on time."[50] This was true for Jesus' disciples, it was true for Lazarus, and it is true for us as well.

Reflection: Has there been an "image of hope" that you hold on to during difficult times in your life? What is it about that image that keeps you going?

---

[49] Raymond E. Brown, *The Anchor Bible: The Gospel According to John (I-XII)* (Garden City, NY: S.S. Doubleday & Company, Inc., 1966), 424.
[50] James Baldwin, *The Fire Next Time* (Modern Library, 2021).

Day 38 • JOHN 11:16

The columnist and author David Brooks wrote a book a few years ago entitled *The Road to Character*. In it, he compares the difference between what he calls resume virtues to eulogy virtues. The former tells people about your skills, while the latter is focused on who you are. Based on the two separate accounts of creation in Genesis, he then refers to our career-oriented nature as Adam 1 and our morally focused nature as Adam 2.

He says, "Adam 1 wants to build, create, produce, and discover things...Adam 2 wants to embody certain moral qualities...[he] wants to love intimately, to sacrifice self in the service of others, to live in obedience to some transcendent truth."[51] Our problem is we are caught between these two natures. We live in a society that stresses resume-building, Adam 1 virtues, but we will inevitably miss out on a certain depth to life if we ignore introspective Adam 2 virtues.

On the other hand, the Apostle Thomas may be a category unto himself. He is brutally honest and typically shoots from the hip. He is impulsive and direct, like Adam 1, but he is also loyal and willing to sacrifice himself, like Adam 2. He is so much more than a "doubter." He is a force to be reckoned with.

When he hears Jesus say they are heading back to hostile Judea for a man who is already dead, he can't help but give his two cents. All the others are silent, even loudmouth Peter, but not Thomas. And what he says is not words of doubt but words of faith. There's no question *if* he's going with Jesus. "Pick up your bags. Let's go," he pretty much says.

But we don't know exactly *how* Thomas said this foreboding sentence. Scholars are split on the matter. Was Realist Thomas resigned to the fact they might die, or was this an act of leadership to rally the others to have courage? It all depends on the tone you use while reading.

It is clear they are heading back into dangerous territory, which may cost them. Following Jesus usually does. We saw the social cost the seeing man in John 9 paid for his profound faith in Jesus. He was kicked out of the synagogue and, thus, essentially, the whole community. Undoubtedly, the disciples had already paid a hefty price for following Jesus for three years. They had walked away from their families and livelihoods to travel with this rabbi from Nazareth. This trip to Judea would just be added to the already long list of sacrifices they made.

[51] David Brooks, *The Road to Character* (Random House Trade Paperbacks, 2015), xii.

Dietrich Bonhoeffer once wrote, "When Christ calls a man, he bids a man come and die."[52] There is much we must give up when we follow Jesus. We must let our self-centered Adam 1 nature go if we are to live into Christ's call. But Thomas and the others didn't realize it was not any of them who would die but Jesus. This trip back to Judea, and ultimately his death, would not be the end of Jesus' ministry but its fulfillment.

We can be confident Jesus would not ask us for anything he has not already gone through. There is a cost to discipleship, but we can be courageous as we live into that cost. We can even be forthright (and a little blunt) like Thomas as we follow Jesus.

Reflection: Over your life, have you aspired to be more like Adam 1 or Adam 2? How has following Jesus affected that?

---

[52] Dietrich Bonhoeffer, *The Cost of Discipleship* (Touchstone Books, 1995).

Day 39 • JOHN 11:17-27

In place of a processional hymn during Episcopal funerals, the priest will read short Scripture passages while walking down the center aisle. It is a stark but powerful moment in the service. It is so different from our other services that it usually grabs the congregation's attention. The very first words out of the priest's mouth come from our lesson today:
"I am Resurrection and I am Life, says the Lord.
Whoever has faith in me shall have life,
even though he die.
And everyone who has life,
and has committed himself to me in faith,
shall not die for ever."[53]

Jesus said these words to Martha, Lazarus' grieving sister. He has finally made his way to Bethany, and by now, Lazarus has been lying in his tomb for four days. Rabbinic tradition taught that a soul lingered around the body for three days but then left on the fourth. The point is Lazarus isn't just dead…he's really dead. Even if there was a slight chance of hope Jesus could do something (anything), the cold grip of death has now set in.

The sisters had patiently waited for Jesus to arrive, even if it was only to say goodbye to his dying friend, but days passed, and still no Jesus. "How long?" they kept asking themselves. "How long until he will come to hear our cry?"

The sisters may have prayed Psalm 40 while they waited for Jesus. "I waited patiently for the LORD; he inclined to me and heard my cry. He drew me up from the pit of destruction, out of the miry bog, and set my feet upon a rock, making my steps secure" (Psalm 40:1–2).

They had waited patiently but to no avail; Lazarus was four days in the grave—dead as a doornail.

Jesus' comment to Martha is astounding when you think about the situation. There is so much grief and pain shared by all who have gathered to mourn, and Jesus talks about resurrection and life. Not as a future promise, as Martha assumes, but as a present reality embodied in who he is.

---

[53] *Book of Common Prayer* (Church Publications, 1979), 491.

Jesus is singing a new song in death's house. The power of death does not have the final say when Jesus is on the scene. And Lazarus' death is not an eternal death, just as Jesus' once-and-for-all death means we are not condemned to an eternal death either. Resurrection can and will be a present reality in and through Jesus.

Does Martha believe this? Jesus pointedly asks her so. She does not answer that question but goes a step further. She proclaims he is the Messiah, the Son of God. Yet again, in John's Gospel, we have a profession of faith, but out of all of them, this is the climatic one: "the Son of God, who is coming into the world" (v. 27). In the Gospel of John, we are taught the main way we can love Jesus is by trusting him. And yet again, it is a woman who makes this bold claim to faith. The next time this happens, it will be Mary Magdalene at the empty tomb.

For those of us who have lost a loved one, we must hold on to Jesus' word ever so dearly. When all seems lost, when it appears death has won, may we hear our Savior's promise, "I am Resurrection, and I am Life."

Reflection: What do Psalm 40 and John 11 teach us about God's purposes for us through all the seasons of life?

Day 40 • JOHN 11:28-37

Not too long ago, a friend of mine went on a beach vacation with his family. On one particular evening, a few of them walked along the beach before a storm was supposed to roll in later that night. As they strolled down the coast, one of his adult sons walked alongside them in the water. The waves were crashing more forcefully as the storm churned in the distance, but no one thought anything of it.

As they kept walking, they chatted about what was for dinner and their plans for the next day. But then they looked over, and suddenly, the young man was gone. Frantically, they called out his name. He was just there walking with them in the water, they kept saying to themselves. Fear took hold of them as they realized a wave must've knocked him down, and a rip current dragged him away from the coast. It was getting dark as the gray clouds continued to roll. They broke up into two groups and headed in opposite directions down the beach, calling his name and asking beachgoers if they had seen him. Hours passed with no sight of the young man. Lifeguards and police were of little help because of the violent waves now crashing on the beach.

Night had set in, and so had the possibility my friend had just lost his son. He walked away from the search party and went down to the far end of the beach alone. He cried out for his son, but then he fell to his knees and cried out to God. In utter anguish and despair, he let out the most heart-wrenching sob from the depths of his soul. Was this the end? How could he go on?

As he picked himself up and kept walking, a stranger ran up to him and said a man was lying on the beach about fifty yards away. He ran in that direction and found his boy, lying on the beach, breathing, thank God. He had been in the water for hours, but somehow, he washed up on the beach. Exhausted and dehydrated, the paramedics rushed him to the hospital, and he spent over a week in the ICU. His lungs had been overextended, but he was alive.

My friend told me this story with tears in his eyes. He described that moment of desperation as "the desolate pit" the psalmist talks about (Psalm 40:2). It was a moment of utter dread and hopelessness. In the end, his son was given back to him, but that memory of utter despair has stayed fresh in his mind.

"Blessed are those who mourn, for they shall be comforted" (Matthew 5:4).

Jesus has a deep and abiding love for those who are heartbroken. In our passage today, he specifically calls for Mary. While her sister ran to Jesus, Mary stayed in the house. She was likely hurt that Jesus didn't come sooner and was overcome by her sorrow. Of the two sisters, Mary is the introvert and had spent days internalizing all this pain. Where Martha needed to talk it out with others, Mary spent all her mental energy asking herself why this happened to her beloved brother.

And then Jesus calls her by name. He calls all the heartbroken, the depressed, and the sorrowful by name.

"Blessed are you who weep now, for you shall laugh" (Luke 6:21).
Even the Son of God is overcome by the reality of death and the toll it has taken on his good friends. He can see the pain so clearly on their faces. He asks to be shown where Lazarus has been laid, and they reply, "Come and see." This term, which John used consistently as an invitation to come and see Jesus and the mighty works he has done, is now presented to him so that he can see the great tragedy of death.

They invite him to come and see, not to come and conquer. For them, death has won; the miracle worker has met his match. But little do they know what the man who was just weeping was about to do. Though he grieves with the rest of them at the reality of death, it will not be a reality for long.

Jesus is moved to act because of his compassion and deep love for Lazarus. He is a God who sees us in our sorrow and even meets us in "the pit." He did it for his friend, and he will to do for us as well.

Reflection: As the baptized, we not only meet others in the pit, but we may find ourselves there, too. How has Jesus met you in these tough moments?

Day 41 • JOHN 11:38-42

"He stinketh."

There is not a better line in all the King James Bible. But it is quite telling that Martha is concerned about the odor. Moments ago, she professed Jesus as the Son of God, and she heard Jesus say he was the resurrection and the life. But at his command to move the tombstone, she falters. "Yes, Jesus is the Messiah, but why would you open the tomb? Death has won. All you must do is smell it!"

She embodies the request made by another person in the Gospels, "I believe; help my unbelief" (Mark 9:24). It seems unthinkable to open the tomb. She thought Jesus was going to pay his respects, not do a full examination of the corpse. She even reminds Jesus it's been four days. In line with their customs, Lazarus' soul was gone for good.

But Jesus doesn't chastise her for this apparent lack of faith. Instead, he reminds her to trust that God will reveal his glory in this tragic situation. God has been glorified with each miracle he has done, one building on top of another. The blind man receiving his sight was a great example of that, but nothing will compare with what was about to happen.

In the next moment, we see Jesus lifting his eyes to the sky. We then hear his heartfelt prayer to his heavenly Father. And in it, we are reminded God always hears our prayers. Our God is not distracted by other things. He attentively listens to us just as he listened to Jesus. There is confidence in this prayer, an assurance that God the Father is not sleeping on the job. He is with Jesus and will work through him to bring life out of death.

Where Martha's faith is weak, Jesus' assurance fills in the gap. But isn't this always the case for Christians? We stumble even in our strongest moments of faith. Like Martha, Peter proclaimed Jesus as Christ and, the next moment, rebuked him. We are weak and desperately need Jesus' strength to be a faithful disciple.

Paul knew this all too well when he said:
"But [the Lord] said to me, 'My grace is sufficient for you, for my power is made perfect in weakness.' Therefore I will boast all the more gladly of my weaknesses, so that the power of Christ may rest upon me. For the sake of

Christ, then, I am content with weaknesses, insults, hardships, persecutions, and calamities. For when I am weak, then I am strong" (2 Corinthians 12:9–11).

We must recognize the frailty of our faith and lean on the One who offers "blessed assurance," as the old hymn goes. What should be a source of comfort is Jesus is always interceding on our behalf. At the very heart of the Trinity is a deep and abiding love that is the Father, Son, and Holy Spirit. The Son only requests what accords with the Father's will. The Father is always graciously giving, and the Holy Spirit enacts and enables the perfect, divine will of them all.

When we admit our weakness and moments of unbelief, we then have access to our Lord in a way we didn't before. Humility is a great doorway into God's heart. We are all Martha, sitting outside the tomb in disbelief. May we have the ears to hear our Lord say, even in the most challenging situations, "I am the resurrection, and I am the life."

Reflection: What are those things in our life that "stinketh"? How might the Lord bring new life to things that have died within ourselves and the communities where we reside?

Day 42 • JOHN 11:43-45

C.S. Lewis's *The Chronicles of Narnia* is a classic children's series that has been a great source of strength in my life. Though it was written for children, it is anything but childish. Lewis was a master at conveying deep theological truths in a way a child could grasp. Now in adulthood, I can marvel at how poignant he is in teaching the faith to young and old alike.

At the end of *The Lion, the Witch and the Wardrobe*, the Christ-figure, Aslan, rises from the dead after sacrificially laying down his life. As the two young girls, Lucy and Susan, discover that he is alive, Aslan has an intimate conversation with them as he regains his strength. He tells them of the deep magic that was formed at the dawn of time that allowed for death to be undone if an innocent victim was killed on the Stone Table. This deep magic broke the White Witch's curse.

After Aslan told the girls this, he looked at them and said the first order of business was for him to let out a mighty roar.

Lewis writes, "And Aslan stood up, and when he opened his mouth to roar, his face became so terrible that they did not dare to look at it. And they saw all the trees in front of him bend before the blast of his roaring as grass bends in a meadow before the wind."[54]

It was a resurrection roar, and it called out to all of creation that evil and death had been vanquished.

I get the same feeling when Jesus cried with a loud voice, "Lazarus, come out." Those words had the power to raise a dead man in the same way God's word created light in the beginning. Jesus' words had the power to create and the power to restore. As the Good Shepherd, he knows his sheep, and he calls them by name. "Lazarus, my beloved friend, come out of there!"

In John's Gospel, this is the seventh and final miracle Jesus performs. It is the climactic moment in his public ministry, foreshadowing what will come. Death is put on notice; it will not reign freely any longer. There is One greater than death on the scene, and he is the "Strong Man" who has come to take back what is rightfully his. He is the true Lord of this world—he is the Lord of life.

[54] C.S. Lewis, *The Chronicles of Narnia: The Lion the Witch and the Wardrobe* (Harper Collins Publishers, 2001), 185.

Jesus commands those around the tomb to unbind Lazarus and let him go. And that really is what life in Christ offers each of us. By the power of the life-giving God, we are released from the dominion of sin and death and free to live into the fullness of God's purposes for us. Jesus frees us from the slavery of sin, and we are called into the newness of life. This is at the heart of baptismal living. As we have said in this book, we go into those waters and die with Christ and are raised in newness of life. By the grace of our baptism, we are all Lazarus in a sense. Jesus has called each of us by name and said, "Come up and out of those baptismal waters. I have unbound you from your sin."

If Nicodemus wanted to know what it meant to be born again, I hope he was in Bethany on that fateful day. New life comes from the Lord of life and him alone. Our story ends much as it began. John tells us that many who witnessed this great miracle believed in Jesus. They are like the Samaritan village that not only marveled but went a step further and believed he was the Messiah. They are like the seeing man, who had experienced firsthand the goodness of the Lord. The baptized are inheritors of the faith of those who have gone before. They stand in a long line of people like Martha, Mary, Lazarus, and others whose lives Jesus forever changed. Once you've heard his resurrection roar, it gets deep in your bones.

As we close with this study, I can't help but think about the two brothers I talked about in Week 3. Their early years were marked by a broken family, but at the moment in their baptism when the congregation welcomed them into the household of God, they couldn't help but weep at the Good News they received. They had become members of a new family with more brothers and sisters than they could count in heaven and on Earth.

May we never forget the charge given to us as we are welcomed into this gracious household: "Confess the faith of Christ crucified, proclaim his resurrection, and share with us in his eternal priesthood."[55]

My friends, or should I say, my dear brothers and sisters, may you know the purpose and power of your baptism. Because of Jesus' death and resurrection, you belong, and may you share in Jesus' mighty resurrection roar.

Reflection: What do you think was Lazarus' response to being raised? How do you think he lived his life after the fact?

---

[55] *Book of Common Prayer* (Church Publications, 1979), 308.

study guide

using this study guide

HOW TO GET THE MOST OUT OF THIS STUDY

As with any individual or small group study of God's Word, you largely reap what you sow—or, as it is commonly put, you get out of it what you put into it. But additionally, there are guidelines that can help you get the most from the efforts you put in. I have outlined some suggestions here for you and your group to review before you get started.

1. Review the Table of Contents. The section entitled "Small Group Leader Helps" lays out best practices for how to host and facilitate a healthy small group and avoid common mistakes. It's a great idea to review this material before having your first meeting.

2. This book is a tool for facilitation. Adapt it to the needs of your group. If a line of discussion leads to green pastures outside the scope of the book, enjoy the leading of the Good Shepherd. Feel free to ask, or allow other members to ask, insightful questions as the Holy Spirit leads.

3. There is a lot of material here. You do not have to ask every question in your group discussion. Feel free to skip questions as needed and linger over the ones where there is authentic conversation.

4. Enjoy the experience. Christian community should be characterized by joy and love. Encourage yourself and the group members to bear such fruit. Pray before each session—ask God to minister to you, the facilitator, and every group member by name. Pray for the discussion, the fellowship, and the personal application.

5. Read the "Outline of Each Session" on the following pages so you understand the flow of the session and how the study works.

outline of each week

OPENING AND CLOSING PRAYER

Begin and end each session with prayer. Invite God into the midst of your conversation. Use the prayers provided or offer one of your own. The prayers provided could be offered by a member of the group or you could all say them together. Close your group with an offer to pray with one another. There is a prayer journal on p. 138 where you can keep track of prayer requests and God's answers to your prayers.

KEY VERSE

Each session begins with a key verse. This verse is a key to understanding the entire week's theme. You may want to memorize these verses. By committing portions of God's Word to long-term memory, you will always have them to refer to, even when you don't have a Bible with you.

COME TO THE FONT

As we gather, a couple of questions are offered to rekindle the fire of our faith in God and mutual trust in one another. Use the opening questions as an opportunity to reconnect each week and re-engage in the discussion.

DAILY DEVOTIONALS

Studying the redeeming promises of the word is like mining a rich vein of gold. The deeper you dig, the more treasure you will discover. Set aside time to spend with the Lord each day. The devotionals will stimulate your personal interaction with God and his Word. Pray and ask the Lord to reveal himself to you through the pages of his Word.

WASHED IN THE WORD

Christians leak. As many times as we have heard the precious and great promises of God, we need continual reminding. The video teachings and assigned group Scripture reading are there to help us focus on the promises of the week and hear again about God's covenant love.

The video segment will provide teaching on the passage and direction for the session, serving as a launchpad for your discussion. You can watch this video ahead of the meeting as individuals, or if possible, watch it as a group. If you are hosting this group as an online group and are experiencing diminished quality, you may need to encourage members to take time to watch the video on their own rather than try to play it through your online meeting platform.

The "Video Notes" section offers summaries of key points from the video teaching. You may want to ask the group a simple question after the video, something like: "What resonated with you from that video teaching?"

There will also be a section of Scripture for the group to read aloud. Questions will follow to help group members make observations and interpret the text. Use as many or as few of these questions as prove helpful.

RENEW THE COVENANT

As we hear God's Word together, we are called to respond by being drawn into deeper trust of God and one another. The second section of every study will seek to call your hearts to greater intimacy and vulnerability with God and your brothers and sisters in Christ. The questions in this section will invite you to apply what you are learning through fellowship, prayer, and corporate worship.

week 1 PRACTICING RIGHTEOUSNESS

OPENING PRAYER

"Almighty and everlasting God, you hate nothing you have made and forgive the sins of all who are penitent: Create and make in us new and contrite hearts, that we, worthily lamenting our sins and acknowledging our wretchedness, may obtain of you, the God of all mercy, perfect remission and forgiveness; through Jesus Christ our Lord, who lives and reigns with you and the Holy Spirit, one God, for ever and ever. Amen." *Book of Common Prayer*, p 217

> *"Your kingdom come, your will be done, on earth as it is in heaven."* — **MATTHEW 6:10**

INTRODUCTION

The baptized are called into a way of life, a mode of being. We see a fuller picture of Jesus' vision for the faithful in his Sermon on the Mount. Matthew 6 gives us a part of that. With this newfound faith also comes a way to live. Jesus' life and words make, it clear not to act like "the hypocrites." Then, like now, plenty of people used religion to showcase themselves in different forms. Unfortunately, nothing has changed.

But Jesus doesn't leave us with the negative; rather, he shows us the way of his kingdom. It is one of thankfulness, simplicity, and generosity. He ultimately summed it up in the only prayer he ever taught his disciples. We can glean so much from this simple prayer that has been passed down through the generations. Offering wisdom without measure, it is usually one of the first prayers we learn as a child and the last one we pray before taking our final breath. It reminds us our heavenly Father loves us and provides for us, and we pray we do his will on earth as it is in heaven.

Our fascination and obsession with social media speaks to the heart of our need for attention and praise. Jesus understands this deep need and hunger inside each of us, but he directs us to our Father, who pours his love and attention on us. His attention truly matters, because it fills us. Therefore, we retreat in secret knowing the Father will gladly meet us there and give us what we truly need.

COME TO THE FONT

1. Do you like to be the center of attention? How does being an introvert or extrovert shape your desire to be seen and known by others?
2. What is your relationship with social media? How has it helped you connect with others? What does it lack?

VIDEO NOTES

In the heart of his Sermon on the Mount, Jesus calls us to shape our behavior to reflect the kingdom of God—that kingdom he was bringing about by his very presence on earth. He teaches us in Matthew 6 how to give and pray.

Give to the needy in secret, go behind closed doors to pray, and when you pray—don't keep going on and on as some do—God's listening from the very start. God doesn't need our prayers. But for some strange reason, he still desperately wants to hear from us.

When we live out our calling as the baptized, that means our priorities must shift and change. We must put all the things we were giving our time and attention to into the perspective of Jesus' call on our life. There are demands on the baptized, and what we are called to is quiet discipleship.

What may be one of the most radical things of all is Jesus teaches us a prayer that will ultimately shape our actions; a prayer that can lead us to be more forgiving, more thankful, and more willing to trust that God is not only our great Provider but that he is, in fact, "our Father (who art in heaven)."

READ MATTHEW 6:1-21

What resonated with you from that video? What was a new insight?

WASHED IN THE WORD

1. Why is secrecy so important to Jesus?
2. Many times, Jesus' teaching can be vague or indirect. Why do you think he gives such specific instructions in this passage?
3. Did anything about the Lord's Prayer stick out to you after seeing it in Jesus' larger argument in Matthew 6?

RENEW THE COVENANT

1. Who is someone who has modeled "quiet discipleship" for you over the years?
2. How can we share the good news of Jesus while also keeping in mind Jesus' call for secrecy?
3. In what ways can you better lay up treasures in heaven going forward?

CLOSING PRAYER

You may want to share prayer requests with one another. There's a Prayer and Praise Journal found on p. 138 where you can keep track of your group's requests. Have someone close in prayer or pray the following prayer together:

"O God, you have taught us to keep all your commandments by loving you and our neighbor: Grant us the grace of your Holy Spirit, that we may be devoted to you with our whole heart, and united to one another with pure affection; through Jesus Christ our Lord, who lives and reigns with you and the Holy Spirit, one God, for ever and ever. *Amen.*" *Book of Common Prayer, p 230, Proper 9*

DAILY DEVOTIONS

Studying the redeeming promises of The Word is like mining a rich vein of gold. The deeper you dig, the more treasure you will discover. Set aside time to spend with the Lord each day. The devotionals will stimulate your personal interaction with God and his Word. Pray and ask the Lord to reveal himself to you through the pages of it.

week 2 — TEMPTATION AND REPENTANCE

OPENING PRAYER

"Almighty God, whose blessed Son was led by the Spirit to be tempted by Satan: Come quickly to help us who are assaulted by many temptations; and, as you know the weaknesses of each of us, let each one find you mighty to save; through Jesus Christ your Son our Lord, who lives and reigns with you and the Holy Spirit, one God, now and for ever. *Amen.*" *Book of Common Prayer 218*

> *"For it is written, 'You shall worship the Lord your God and him only shall you serve.'"*
> — **MATTHEW 4:10**

INTRODUCTION

Millions of people have followed the twelve-step program for a reason. That's because it works. It isn't a self-help program that promises success after a certain number of days, nor does it promise happiness and fulfillment with three easy steps. Its true gift is its brutal honesty. It forces people to look at themselves honestly and accept they will always and forever be a work in progress on this side of eternity. We are all works in progress, whether we've joined the recovery community or not. They just know the secret.

But this makes the incarnation and temptation of Jesus even more amazing. Jesus didn't need to do all this, but he did it anyway because of us. He goes into the wilderness and faces evil head-on, and like a boxer who absorbs one blow after another, he comes out victorious. He has fought back the tempter with faith. He, the Logos, has held onto the Word of God, and it proved to be the North Star guiding him in the challenging moments of temptation.

Temptation is a human predicament that none of us have figured out a way to avoid. Not even Jesus avoids it, but he faces it head-on with faith that God's Word is true and sure. The temptations prove to us there is a battle for the human heart. As the baptized, we have been given a new identity, and we must not be lured into being agents of sin and death any longer. We are under new management. We are the Lord's, and faith in him can overcome even the wiles of the evil one.

COME TO THE FONT

1. When you think of the devil, what comes to mind?
2. What are some things you love? To what do you give your time, attention, and resources?

VIDEO NOTES

The story of Jesus' temptation is connected to his baptism. We cannot forget that after John baptized Jesus, the Spirit led Jesus into the wilderness.

Though we aren't given many details about this tempter, one thing is clear: he exists and persists in his goal of destroying God's work in the world. His name in Greek, *diabolos*, can be traced to the verb that means "to split." And if you think about it from the very start of the Bible (Genesis 3), a force is at work to split humanity from their Creator.

This evil force, the great tempter himself, is the one who was actively at work in the wilderness against Jesus and is actively working to come between God and us as well.

Being rooted in Scripture is essential as is good interpretation of Scripture. The devil twists the Bible for his own means, but Jesus continually corrects Satan's bad interpretation.

Jesus is with us—full stop. He's there to show us the way into baptism, and he is there to guide us out of those dark moments of temptation.

READ MATTHEW 4:1–11

What resonated with you from that video? What was a new insight?

WASHED IN THE WORD

1. Refer to Matthew 3:13–17. Why do you think Jesus' baptism and temptation happened back-to-back?
2. What do you notice about the progression of the three temptations?
3. What does verse 11 say about Jesus' humanity? What strength might that give us?

RENEW THE COVENANT

1. What are some temptations with which we all struggle, no matter who we are?
2. What has helped you in moments of temptation?
3. We are what we love, and we worship in one form or fashion what we love. So how does worship of God play a part in forming our desires?

CLOSING PRAYER

You may want to share prayer requests with one another. There's a Prayer and Praise Journal found on p. 138 where you can keep track of your group's requests. Have someone close in prayer or pray the following prayer together:

"Almighty God, you know that we have no power in ourselves to help ourselves: Keep us both outwardly in our bodies and inwardly in our souls, that we may be defended from all adversities which may happen to the body, and from all evil thoughts which may assault and hurt the soul; through Jesus Christ our Lord, who lives and reigns with you and the Holy Spirit, one God, for ever and ever. Amen." *Book of Common Prayer, p 218*

DAILY DEVOTIONS

Studying the redeeming promises of The Word is like mining a rich vein of gold. The deeper you dig, the more treasure you will discover. Set aside time to spend with the Lord each day. The devotionals will stimulate your personal interaction with God and his Word. Pray and ask the Lord to reveal himself to you through the pages of it.

week 3   BE BORN AGAIN

OPENING PRAYER

"O God, you prepared your disciples for the coming of the Spirit through the teaching of your Son Jesus Christ: Make the hearts and minds of your servants ready to receive the blessing of the Holy Spirit, that they may be filled with the strength of his presence; through Jesus Christ our Lord. Amen." *Book of Common Prayer, p 819*

> *"Truly, truly, I say to you, unless one is born of water and the Spirit, he cannot enter the kingdom of God. That which is born of the flesh is flesh, and that which is born of the Spirit is spirit."* — JOHN 3:5-6

INTRODUCTION

Being shrouded in darkness can be an unsettling feeling, especially if you find yourself in an unfamiliar place. Just think about being lost in the woods in the dead of night. It's likely the last place you want to be. At the same time, the darkness can also be a safe haven for those who want their actions concealed. You can dart back and forth without anyone realizing you're there. It is no wonder Nicodemus comes to Jesus in the dead of night, hidden from prying eyes. If he was caught with this rabbi from Nazareth, his position of authority could be thrown into question.

Over the course of their conversation, Jesus shows Nicodemus his faith is lacking the true light of all. Nothing could be more unsettling than to realize you're unknowingly living in darkness. Extreme action is required, and Jesus' answer to that predicament is the need for new birth. It is utterly drastic and absolutely necessary in Jesus' eyes.

With this earth-shaking news, Jesus invites Nicodemus into his light. It may not happen instantly, but he is called to step out of the darkness and into the light of faith—a faith that claims Jesus was sent into the world out of God's great love for his creation. Or as he heard it that night, "For God so loved the world, that he gave his only Son."

COME TO THE FONT

1. When you hear the phrase "born again," what comes to mind?
2. How does the particular religious background we grew up in shape how we understand and engage with different aspects of our faith today?

VIDEO NOTES

The deep and lasting life Christ offers is for those who "believe in him." Faith is a gift from God and our grateful response to God's action. He has brought about our victory and redemption "while we were yet sinners," as Paul says in Romans.

Tertullian once said, "Christians are made, not born." Even if we're born into a Christian family, that doesn't automatically mean we are Christians, too. Baptism is our doorway into this new life in Christ. Though we may inherit many great qualities from our parents, we must embrace the faith for ourselves. No one may claim the Christian faith as a birthright.

New birth requires a willing and open heart to this transformational power of God—a power that far exceeds our wildest imaginations. It can bring light out of the darkness, healing out of brokenness, and salvation to all who long to draw closer to the Source of this magnificent splendor.

READ JOHN 3:1-17

What resonated with you from that video? What was a new insight?

WASHED IN THE WORD

1. What do you think motivated Nicodemus to visit Jesus in the first place? Why take that risk?
2. What is the hardest or most challenging part of Jesus' answer in that passage for you? What are you still wondering about after reading it?
3. Looking at verse 14, what is the argument Jesus is trying to make? Refer to the Day 20 devotion for more details.

RENEW THE COVENANT

1. Do you equate being born again and baptism as the same thing, or are they somehow different? How has either or both shaped your faith today?
2. In what ways is God inviting you out of the darkness and into his light?
3. If God loved the world so much to send his Son, then we can be confident God loves us that much as well. How does God's love give us hope and purpose in our life?

CLOSING PRAYER

You may want to share prayer requests with one another. There's a Prayer and Praise Journal found on p. 138 where you can keep track of your group's requests. Have someone close in prayer or pray the following prayer together:

"O God, whose glory it is always to have mercy: Be gracious to all who have gone astray from your ways, and bring them again with penitent hearts and steadfast faith to embrace and hold fast the unchangeable truth of your Word, Jesus Christ your Son; who with you and the Holy Spirit lives and reigns, one God, for ever and ever. *Amen.*" *Book of Common Prayer p. 218*

DAILY DEVOTIONS

Studying the redeeming promises of The Word is like mining a rich vein of gold. The deeper you dig, the more treasure you will discover. Set aside time to spend with the Lord each day. The devotionals will stimulate your personal interaction with God and his Word. Pray and ask the Lord to reveal himself to you through the pages of it.

week 4 — LIVING WATER

OPENING PRAYER

"Everliving God, whose will it is that all should come to you through your Son Jesus Christ: Inspire our witness to him, that all may know the power of his forgiveness and the hope of his resurrection; who lives and reigns with you and the Holy Spirit, one God, now and for ever. *Amen.*" *Book of Common Prayer, p 816–817*

> "But the hour is coming, and is now here, when the true worshipers will worship the Father in spirit and truth, for the Father is seeking such people to worship him. God is spirit, and those who worship him must worship in spirit and truth."
>
> — JOHN 4:23-24

INTRODUCTION

In the beautiful chapel of The University of the South, the font is placed in the center aisle. This isn't unusual for many churches want to make the point we all come through the waters of baptism and then are led to the Eucharistic feast. It serves as a visual symbol of a theological point. What makes this font memorable is the water in the font is moving. It was a requirement that ancient Jewish ritual baths had moving water, or what they called living water.

Jesus offers the Samaritan woman in John 4 living water, but little does she know this water is not physically moving or physical at all; rather, she will be spiritually moved by it. Like a mighty river, this living water Jesus offers is a gift he graciously gives to all those who thirst for something more, something he alone can offer.

We will not be bound by location with this spiritual water. Our Jerusalems or Samarias will only be of secondary concern, for the Lord will be principally worshipped in "spirit and truth." This water is as much for the outsider as it is the insider. It transcends boundaries, in part because it is always on the move and looking for those who are thirsting for it.

COME TO THE FONT

1. Where is a place you feel close to God? What makes that place special to you?

2. When have you found yourself in an "us" vs. "them" mentality? It could be sports, politics, etc. What does that mentality teach us about humanity?

VIDEO NOTES

The Samaritan woman's encounter with Jesus is a wonderful surprise and an unexpected crossing of paths in the Gospel narrative. Jesus meets this woman and needs a drink. He, the Messiah, puts himself lower than the woman and needs her help. But what begins as a conversation about literal water turns into Jesus' teaching about spiritual water that lasts—a teaching rooted in the ancient prophets of Israel.

The prophet Ezekiel says, "And wherever the river goes, every living creature that swarms will live, and there will be very many fish. For this water goes there, that the waters of the sea may become fresh; so everything will live where the river goes" (47:9).

This Samaritan woman came to the well for some water, but after encountering Jesus, she transformed into a gushing well of living water herself. She becomes a preacher and missionary in the same town that designated her as an outsider. And quite shockingly, the town comes to faith in Jesus. A trickle becomes a mighty river of living water...and it happened in Samaria.

READ JOHN 4:5-42

What resonated with you from that video? What was a new insight?

WASHED IN THE WORD

1. Consider Ezekiel 47 and what Jesus himself says about the topic in our passage, what actually is this water he offers?
2. Is the woman comforted that Jesus knows her life history or terrified? Do you find it comforting that Jesus knows everything about each of us?
3. Why do you think the Samaritan village so quickly accepted the woman's testimony about Jesus?

RENEW THE COVENANT

1. What are some things you long (or thirst) for?
2. Who are the outsiders (i.e., Samaritans) in your life? How might God be inviting you into a new perspective about those people? What might he be calling you into?
3. How might you live out the missionary spirit of the Samaritan woman in your community?

CLOSING PRAYER

You may want to share prayer requests with one another. There's a Prayer and Praise Journal found on p. 138 where you can keep track of your group's requests. Have someone close in prayer or pray the following prayer together:

"Almighty God, you alone can bring into order the unruly wills and affections of sinners: Grant your people grace to love what you command and desire what you promise; that, among the swift and varied changes of the world, our hearts may surely there be fixed where true joys are to be found; through Jesus Christ our Lord, who lives and reigns with you and the Holy Spirit, one God, now and for ever. *Amen.*" *Book of Common Prayer, p 219*

DAILY DEVOTIONS

Studying the redeeming promises of The Word is like mining a rich vein of gold. The deeper you dig, the more treasure you will discover. Set aside time to spend with the Lord each day. The devotionals will stimulate your personal interaction with God and his Word. Pray and ask the Lord to reveal himself to you through the pages of it.

week 5 NEW EYES

OPENING PRAYER

"O God of peace, who hast taught us that in returning and rest we shall be saved, in quietness and in confidence shall be our strength: By the might of thy Spirit lift us, we pray thee, to thy presence, where we may be still and know that thou art God; through Jesus Christ our Lord. Amen." *Book of Common Prayer, p 832*

> *"You do not know where he comes from, and yet he opened my eyes... Never since the world began has it been heard that anyone opened the eyes of a man born blind. If this man were not from God, he could do nothing."*
>
> **— JOHN 9:30B, 32–33**

INTRODUCTION

The nursery rhyme, "Three Blind Mice," has a simple tune that even a beginner could master on the piano in a day. This early seventeenth-century song ends, "Did you ever see such a sight in your life, As three blind mice?" The point is, you need a guide who can actually see the way to go. Jesus himself talked of the blind leading the blind, but he is not speaking of physical blindness (Matthew 15:14). As is usually the case in the Gospels, it's the tax collectors, prostitutes, and even the blind who see more clearly than the learned religious leaders. The scribes' and Pharisees' eyesight is just fine, but they are spiritually blind as a bat.

How could Jesus, the mud-maker (aka Sabbath-breaker), be the fulfillment of Isaiah's prophecy that one day God would come "to open eyes that are blind, to free captives from prison and to release from the dungeon those who sit in darkness" (42:7)? As the Pharisees try to rationalize and deny this great miracle out of their fear of what this might mean, the former blind man is the one who truly sees and becomes a teacher to the teachers. He gains courage from his newfound faith, and by the end, he is worshiping Jesus as the Son of Man.

COME TO THE FONT

1. Do you have any phobias, fears, or things you're afraid of that you're willing to share with the group?
2. Would you consider yourself more fearful or courageous? How might that have shaped some decisions you've made in your life? Can you think of a time when you were courageous?

VIDEO NOTES

With each passage in John, we encounter more courage and more faith in people we wouldn't typically expect. We are reminded God works in and through whomever he wants…whenever he wants. That alone is a miracle for us to consider.

Who sinned, and who sees? We all sin, but with Jesus, we are given vision that goes deeper. He shows us the world as it is and what it should be (and will be when he returns).

When we are washed in the spiritual Siloam of Christ, we are given a gift to glimpse the world as the seeing man in John 9 did. It was after the washing in the Pool of Siloam (and not before) that he professed faith in Jesus. For us as well, Jesus gives us this great gift to see him for who he truly is—even if that is years after our baptism. And you and I are called to courageously live out our faith like the seeing man.

READ JOHN 9:1-41

What resonated with you from that video? What was a new insight?

WASHED IN THE WORD

1. What do you make of the disciples' question to Jesus in v. 2? Have you ever asked a similar question to yourself? If so, does this question lead us to believe in some form of karma?
2. Why do you think the formerly blind man's (or the seeing man's) parents acted the way they did?
3. Which of the seeing man's responses in the passage sticks out to you the most? What can we learn from him?

RENEW THE COVENANT

1. It appears the Pharisees and the man's parents are governed first by fear of the unknown. How might we overcome our anxiety and fear with faith in Jesus?
2. Jesus offers new sight to those who have become spiritually blind. How has Jesus changed how you see the world? Where do you still feel you need clearer vision in your life?
3. How might you embody the courage of the seeing man in your life today?

CLOSING PRAYER

You may want to share prayer requests with one another. There's a Prayer and Praise Journal found on p. 138 where you can keep track of your group's requests. Have someone close in prayer or pray the following prayer together:

"Almighty and eternal God, so draw our hearts to thee, so guide our minds, so fill our imaginations, so control our wills, that we may be wholly thine, utterly dedicated unto thee; and then use us, we pray thee, as thou wilt, and always to thy glory and the welfare of thy people; through our Lord and Savior Jesus Christ. Amen." *Book of Common Prayer, p 832–833*

DAILY DEVOTIONS

Studying the redeeming promises of The Word is like mining a rich vein of gold. The deeper you dig, the more treasure you will discover. Set aside time to spend with the Lord each day. The devotionals will stimulate your personal interaction with God and his Word. Pray and ask the Lord to reveal himself to you through the pages of it.

week 6 — DEATH TO LIFE

OPENING PRAYER

"O God, the protector of all who trust in you, without whom nothing is strong, nothing is holy: Increase and multiply upon us your mercy; that, with you as our ruler and guide, we may so pass through things temporal, that we lose not the things eternal; through Jesus Christ our Lord, who lives and reigns with you and the Holy Spirit, one God, for ever and ever. *Amen.*" *Book of Common Prayer, p 231*

> "He cried out with a loud voice, 'Lazarus, come out.' The man who had died came out, his hands and feet bound with linen strips, and his face wrapped with a cloth. Jesus said to them, 'Unbind him, and let him go.'"
>
> — JOHN 11: 43B-44

INTRODUCTION

"Shake your grave clothes off." That's not only the chorus of a song from the band Birdtalker, but it is also the essence of Jesus' call to Lazarus. The echoes of death's ultimate defeat grow louder with each passing chapter in John's Gospel, and nothing sounds the alarms more than the lifeless Lazarus walking out of his tomb and shaking off his grave clothes.

In baptism, we share in Jesus' death, we go into those waters and die with Christ, but we don't stay there forever. We rise with Christ, and the congregation then proclaims in one glorious voice, "We receive you into the household of God. Confess the faith of Christ crucified, proclaim his resurrection, and share with us in his eternal priesthood" (The Book of Common Prayer, p 308).

The great gift of baptism is all these, but most importantly, it is being welcomed into this beloved household. This isn't membership in the local country club; this is the entrance into an eternal family whose members span both heaven and earth. In its ranks are apostles, prophets, and even you and me. Like everything else with Jesus, this is a gift, and one that came at a great cost, but because of his sacrifice, it is freely given to all who long to shake death's grave clothes off and put on the robes of the new creation.

COME TO THE FONT

1. Can you think of a moment when you were utterly shocked because of something good that happened? What was that like?
2. Thinking about the other time we meet Martha and Mary (Luke 10:38–42), which one are you more like and why?

VIDEO NOTES

Baptism is our womb and our tomb. With Nicodemus, we learned about new birth, and with Lazarus, we learned about how Jesus brings life out of death. Remember what Paul said in Romans 6:4, "We were buried therefore with him by baptism into death, in order that, just as Christ was raised from the dead by the glory of the Father, we too might walk in newness of life." In those baptismal waters, we are given a new life, a gift, much like Lazarus was given. The question is, what do we do with that gift?

To be the baptized means to be in the midst of community, to be in the midst of God's family. We very well may be called to be springs of living water as the Samaritan woman or given new sight like the blind man in John 9, but no matter what, we are given a place and a purpose within the gathered people of God—what the New Testament writers liked to call the *ekklesia* (or the church).

READ JOHN 11:1-45

What resonated with you from that video? What was a new insight?

WASHED IN THE WORD

1. Compare and contrast the different reactions of Mary and Martha when Jesus arrives. What do they teach us about different ways to grieve?
2. Is Thomas' reaction hopeless or hopeful in verse 16? What could it teach us about being a disciple?
3. How do you imagine Lazarus lived for the rest of his life?

RENEW THE COVENANT

1. What places in your life could the Lord come and breathe new life?
2. The baptized are called to be a part of a resurrection community. What has this small group experience meant to you and your faith?
3. What will you take away most from this study?

CLOSING PRAYER

You may want to share prayer requests with one another. There's a Prayer and Praise Journal found on p. 138 where you can keep track of your group's requests. Have someone close in prayer or pray the following prayer together:

"Almighty and everliving God, in your tender love for the human race you sent your Son our Savior Jesus Christ to take upon him our nature, and to suffer death upon the cross, giving us the example of his great humility: Mercifully grant that we may walk in the way of his suffering, and also share in his resurrection; through Jesus Christ our Lord, who lives and reigns with you and the Holy Spirit, one God, for ever and ever. Amen." *Book of Common Prayer, p 219*

DAILY DEVOTIONS

Studying the redeeming promises of The Word is like mining a rich vein of gold. The deeper you dig, the more treasure you will discover. Set aside time to spend with the Lord each day. The devotionals will stimulate your personal interaction with God and his Word. Pray and ask the Lord to reveal himself to you through the pages of it.

appendices

frequently asked questions

WHAT DO WE DO ON THE FIRST NIGHT OF OUR GROUP?

Have a party! A "get to know you" coffee, dinner, or dessert is a great way to launch a new study. You may want to review the Small Group Covenant (p. 136) and share the names of a few friends you can invite to join you. But most importantly, have fun before your study time begins.

WHERE DO WE FIND NEW MEMBERS FOR OUR GROUP?

Finding members can be troubling, especially for new groups that have only a few people or for existing groups that have lost a few people along the way. We encourage you to pray with your group and then brainstorm a list of people from work, church, your neighborhood, your children's school, family, the gym, and so forth. Use the five circles to identify potential group members with whom you would like to build a spiritual friendship. Have each group member invite several people on their list.

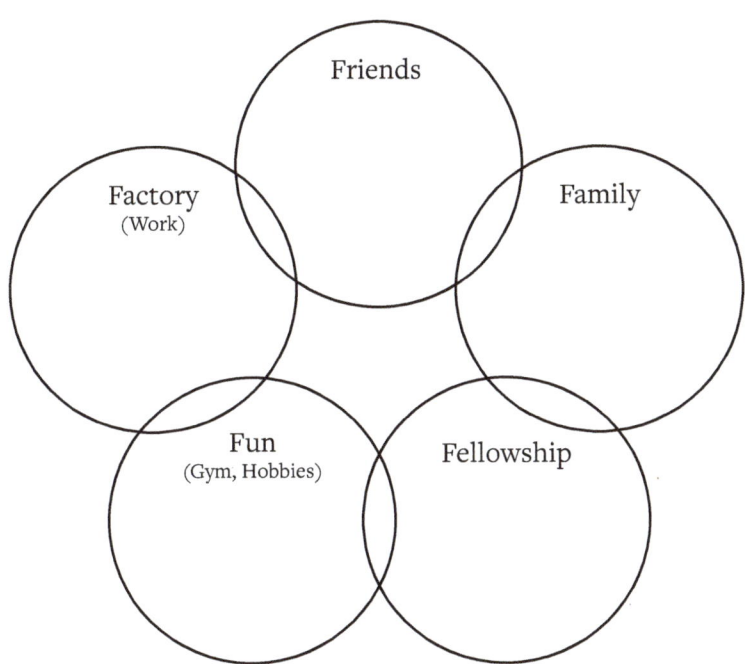

No matter how you find members, it's vital that you stay on the lookout for new people to join your group. All groups tend to go through healthy attrition—the result of moves, sending out new leaders, ministry opportunities, and so forth—and if the group gets too small, it could be at risk of ending. If you and your group stay open to ideas, you'll be amazed at the people God sends your way. The next person just might become a friend for life. You never know!

HOW LONG WILL THIS GROUP MEET?

Most groups meet weekly for at least their first six weeks, but every other week can work as well. We strongly recommend that the group meet for the first six months on a weekly basis if at all possible. This allows for continuity and, if people miss a meeting, they aren't gone for a whole month.

At the end of this study, each group member may decide if they want to continue on for another study. Some groups launch relationships for years to come, and others are stepping-stones into another group experience. Either way, enjoy the journey.

CAN WE DO THIS STUDY ON OUR OWN?

Absolutely! This may sound crazy, but one of the best ways to do this study is not with a full house but with a few friends. You may choose to gather with another couple who would enjoy some relational time (perhaps going to the movies or having a quiet dinner) and then walking through this six-week study. Jesus will be with you even if there are only two of you (Matthew 18:20).

WHO IS THE LEADER?

Most groups have an official leader. But ideally, the group will mature, and members will rotate the leadership of meetings. We have discovered that healthy groups rotate hosts/leaders and homes on a regular basis. This model ensures that all members grow, make their unique contribution, and develop their gifts. This study guide and the Holy Spirit can keep things on track even when you rotate leaders. Christ has promised to be in your midst as you gather. Ultimately, God is your leader each step of the way.

WHAT IF THIS GROUP IS NOT WORKING FOR US?

You're not alone! This could be the result of a personality conflict, life stage difference, geographical distance, level of spiritual maturity, or any number of things. Relax. Pray for God's direction, and at the end of this six-week study, decide whether to continue with this group or find another. You don't typically buy the first car you test drive or marry the first person you date, and the same goes with a group. However, don't bail out before the six weeks are up— God might have something to teach you. Also, don't run from conflict or prejudge people before you have given them a chance. God is still working in your life, too!

HOW DO WE HANDLE THE CHILDCARE NEEDS IN OUR GROUP?

Very carefully. This can be a sensitive issue. We suggest that you empower the group to openly brainstorm solutions. You may try one option that works for a while and then adjust over time. Our favorite approach is for adults to meet in the living room or dining room and to share the cost of a babysitter (or two) who can watch the children in a different part of the house. This way, parents don't have to be away from their children all evening when their children are too young to be left at home. A second option is to use one home for the children and a second home (close by or a phone call away) for the adults. A third idea is to rotate the responsibility of providing a lesson or care for the children either in the same home or in another home nearby. This can be an incredible blessing for young ones. Finally, the most common solution is to decide that you need to have a night to invest in your spiritual lives individually or as a couple and to make your own arrangements for childcare. No matter what decision the group makes, the best approach is to dialogue openly about both the need and the solution.

small group covenant

OUR PURPOSE
To provide a predictable environment where participants experience authentic Christian community to grow spiritually.

GROUP ATTENDANCE
To give priority to the group meeting. We will call or email if we will be late or absent. (Completing the Group Calendar on p. 139 will minimize this issue.)

SAFE ENVIRONMENT
To help create a safe place where people can be heard and feel loved. (Please, no quick answers, snap judgments, or simple fixes.)

RESPECT DIFFERENCES
To be gentle and gracious with different spiritual maturity levels, personal opinions, temperaments, or "imperfections" in fellow group members. We are all works in progress.

CONFIDENTIALITY
To keep anything shared strictly confidential and within the group, and to avoid sharing improper information about those outside the group.

ENCOURAGEMENT FOR GROWTH
To be not just takers, but givers of life. We want to spiritually multiply our lives by serving others with our God-given gifts.

SHARED OWNERSHIP
To remember that every member is a minister and to ensure that each attender will share a small team role or responsibility over time.

ROTATING HOSTS, FACILITATORS, AND HOMES
To encourage different people to host the group in their homes and to rotate the responsibility of facilitating each meeting. (See the Group Calendar on p. 139)

group calendar

Planning and calendaring can help ensure the greatest participation at every meeting. At the end of each meeting, review this calendar. Be sure to include a regular rotation of host homes and facilitator. Don't forget birthdays, socials, church events, holidays, and mission/ministry projects.

Date	Session	Host Home	Snacks	Facilitator
	1			
	2			
	3			
	4			
	5			
	6			

prayer and praise journal

Session 1

Session 2

Session 3

Session 4

Session 5

Session 6

small group roster

Use the chart below to collect names and contact information from all the group members. We suggest one member (other than the host) "own" the task of collecting and distributing the contact info to everyone—via group text message or email—so that people can be in touch.

Name	Email	Cell Phone

small group leader helps

HOSTING AN OPEN HOUSE

If you're starting a new group, try planning an Open House before your first formal group meeting. Even if you have only two to four core members, it's a great way to break the ice and prayerfully consider who else might be open to joining you over the next few weeks. You can also use this kick-off meeting to hand out books, spend some time getting to know each other, discuss each person's expectations for the group, and briefly pray for each other. A simple meal or good dessert always makes a kick-off meeting more fun. After people introduce themselves and share how they ended up at the meeting (you can play a game to see who has the wildest story!), have everyone respond to a few icebreaker questions, such as:

- What is your favorite family vacation?
- What is one thing you love about your church/our community?
- What are two things about your life growing up that most people here don't know?

Next, ask everyone to tell what they hope to get out of the study. You might want to review the Small Group Covenant on p. 136 and discuss each person's expectations and priorities. Finally, set an open chair (maybe two) in the center of your group and explain that it represents someone who would enjoy or benefit from this group who isn't here yet.

Ask people to pray about inviting someone to join the group over the next few weeks. Hand out postcards and have everyone write an invitation or two. Don't worry about having too many people. You can always have one discussion circle in the living room and another in the dining room after you watch the lesson. Each group could then report prayer requests and progress at the end of the session.

You can skip this kick-off meeting if your time is limited, but you'll experience a huge benefit if you take the time to connect with one another in this way.

LEADING FOR THE FIRST TIME

Seven common leadership experiences. Welcome to life out in front!

- **Sweaty palms are a healthy sign.** The Bible says God is gracious to the humble. Remember who is in control; the time to worry is when you're not worried. Those who are soft in heart (and sweaty-palmed) are those whom God is sure to speak through.

- **Seek support.** Ask your leader, co-leader, or a close friend to pray for you and prepare with you before the session. Walking through the study will help you anticipate potentially difficult questions and discussion topics.

- **Bring your uniqueness to the study.** Lean into who you are and how God wants you to lead the study uniquely.

- **Prepare. Prepare. Prepare.** Go through the session, and read the section of Scripture. If you are using the video, listen to the teaching segment. Consider writing in a journal or praying through the day to prepare yourself for what God wants to do. Don't wait until the last minute to prepare.

- **Ask for feedback so you can grow.** Perhaps in an email or on index cards handed out at the study, have everyone write down three things you did well and one thing you could improve on. Don't get defensive. Instead, show an openness to learn and grow.

- **Share with your group what God is doing in your heart.** God is searching for those whose hearts are fully his. Share your trials and victories. We promise that people will relate.

- **Prayerfully consider whom you would like to pass the baton to next week.** It's only fair. God is ready for the next member of your group to go on the faith journey you just traveled. Make it fun, and expect God to do the rest.

leadership training 101

Congratulations! You have responded to the call to help shepherd Jesus' flock. Few other tasks in the family of God surpass the contribution you will be making. As you prepare to lead, whether for one session or the entire series, here are a few thoughts to keep in mind. We encourage you to read and review these with each new discussion leader before they lead.

1. Remember, you are not alone. God knows everything about you, and he knew you would be asked to lead this group. It is common for all good leaders to feel they are not ready to lead. Moses, Solomon, Jeremiah, and Timothy were all reluctant to lead. God promises, *"Never will I leave you; never will I forsake you"* (Hebrews 13:5). Whether you are leading for one evening, several weeks, or a lifetime, you will be blessed as you serve.

2. Don't try to do it alone. Pray right now for God to help you build a healthy leadership team. If you can enlist a co-leader to help you lead the group, you will find your experience much richer. This is your chance to involve as many people as possible in building a healthy group. All you have to do is call and ask people to help. You'll probably be surprised at the response.

3. Just be yourself. If you won't be you, who will? God wants you to use your unique gifts and temperament. Don't try to do things exactly like another leader; do them in a way that fits you! Just admit it when you don't have an answer and apologize when you make a mistake. Your group will love you for it, and you'll sleep better at night!

4. Prepare for your meeting ahead of time. Review the session and write down your responses to each question. Pay special attention to exercises that ask group members to do something other than engage in discussion, like take an action. These exercises will help your group live what the Bible teaches, not just talk about it.

5. Pray for your group members by name. Before you begin your session, go around the room in your mind and pray for each member. Ask God to use your time together to touch every person's heart uniquely. Expect God to lead you to whomever he wants you to encourage or challenge in a special way. If you listen, God will surely lead!

6. When you ask a question, be patient. Someone will eventually respond. Sometimes people need a moment or two of silence to think about the question. Keep in mind, if silence doesn't bother you, it won't bother anyone else. After someone responds, affirm the response with a simple "thanks" or "good job." Then ask, "How about somebody else?" or "Would someone who hasn't shared like to add anything?" Be sensitive to new people or members who aren't ready to say, pray, or do anything. If you give them a safe setting, they will blossom over time.

7. Provide transitions between questions. Always read aloud the transitional paragraphs and questions when guiding the discussion. Ask the group if anyone would like to read the paragraphs or Bible passages. Don't call on anyone, but ask for volunteers; be patient until someone begins. Be sure to thank the people who read aloud.

8. Break up into small groups each week, or a larger group won't stay. If your group has a lot of people, we strongly encourage you to have the group sometimes gather in discussion circles of three or four people during the Renew the Covenant sections. With a greater opportunity to talk in small circles, people will connect more with the study, apply more quickly what they're learning, and ultimately get more out of it. A small circle encourages a quiet person to participate and can minimize the effect of a more dominant or vocal member. It can also help people feel more loved in your group.

When you gather again at the end of the section, you can have one person summarize the highlights from each circle. Small circles are also helpful during prayer time. People uncomfortable with praying aloud will feel more comfortable trying it with just two or three others.

Also, prayer requests won't take as much time, so circles will have more time to pray. When you gather back with the whole group, you can have one person from each circle briefly update everyone on the prayer requests. People are more willing to break into small circles to pray if they know the whole group will hear all the prayer requests.

9. Rotate facilitators weekly. At the end of each meeting, ask the group who should lead the following week. Let the group help select your weekly facilitator. You may be perfectly capable of leading each time, but you will help others grow in their faith and gifts if you give them opportunities to lead. You can use the Small Group Calendar (p. 137) to fill in the names of the different leaders for all the meetings if you prefer.

10. One final challenge (for new or first-time leaders): Before your first opportunity to lead, look up each of the five passages listed below. Read each as a devotional exercise to help equip yourself with a shepherd's heart. Trust us on this one. If you do this, you will be more than ready to lead your first meeting.

Matthew 9:36
1 Peter 5:2-4
Psalm 23
Ezekiel 34:11-16
1 Thessalonians 2:7-8, 11-2

www.ingramcontent.com/pod-product-compliance
Lightning Source LLC
Chambersburg PA
CBHW061800070526
44586CB00023B/2651